PRODUCT OF THE PEOPLE

MARCUS HARVEY

HOW PORTLAND GEAR HARNESSED THE PRIDE OF ROSE CITY

PRODUCT OF THE PEOPLE

COPYRIGHT © 2022 MARCUS HARVEY
All rights reserved.

PRODUCT OF THE PEOPLE
How Portland Gear Harnessed the Pride of Rose City

FIRST EDITION

ISBN   978-1-5445-3610-1 *Hardcover*
       978-1-5445-3611-8 *Paperback*
       978-1-5445-3612-5 *Ebook*

To my beautiful wife, Noelle, who's been with me every step of the way; my sister, Kayla, and her husband, Jonny, for letting me overstay my welcome; and my incredibly supportive parents. I love you all.

CONTENTS

INTRODUCTION 9
1. FAMILY FIRST 15
2. THE CLAWSET 23
3. A MOTHER'S BELIEF 31
4. THE BATHTUB WILL DO 37
5. THE T-SHIRT GUY 43
6. FIRED 51
7. SUCCESSFUL FAILURES 57
8. CAN I STAY A BIT LONGER? 67
9. @PORTLAND 77
10. HACKED 85
11. VALIDATION 95
12. LAUNCH AND LOVE 101
13. BUILDING COMMUNITY 109
14. BRICK AND MORTAR 115
15. LIVING THE DREAM 119
16. FAINTING 125
17. ANXIETY AND INSECURITIES 131
18. WHERE WE ARE 139

INTRODUCTION

AS MY VISION BEGAN TO NARROW, CHEST FEELING HEAVY, lights growing dim, I heard a voice in my head say, Take a deep breath and hang in there. Think of a way to get down lower so when you faint and fall, you won't hurt your head as much when you hit the ground.

I was experiencing my first panic attack and feeling scared I might faint for the third time that month.

As I sat down cross-legged on the cold marble floor in front of three hundred students, in the middle of sharing the Portland Gear story at the University of Portland in 2017, the only excuse I could think to give was, "Sorry everyone—my leg is cramping, and I need to sit down for a second."

I skipped through the remaining slides of my presentation as fast as I could and felt tears welling up in my eyes.

I just wanted to be alone so I could break down and cry.

Just make it through the presentation. You've given this talk over fifty times and love doing it. Hang on.

I kept telling myself this, on repeat.

What would everyone think if the owner of Portland Gear looked weak? How embarrassed would it make me feel? Would they post a video of me fainting on social media and it go viral? What would it do to my reputation? Would anybody still think I was cool?

Still sitting on the floor faking the leg cramp, I made it through the slides and then was able to crawl to a nearby chair.

Normally after I shared my story with students, one or two would stay to chat, but on that spring day nearly forty kids lined up. As I sat in the chair with my head between my knees, experiencing my first full-on panic attack, I tried to catch my breath and smile my way through pictures and questions.

I was spent.

Even though I was surrounded by people, I felt incredibly alone. I couldn't catch my breath, and it seemed like something was broken inside. I'd lived my entire life as a healthy, carefree person; but suddenly it was as if I wasn't in my own body.

I didn't like it.

When the students finally left, all that remained was my confused body and the leader of the business camp, then nineteen-year-old Zack Dean, who looked on with worry.

INTRODUCTION

The second the room cleared, I fell to the ground and started to cry uncontrollably, gasping to catch a breath. I couldn't figure out why this was happening or how to stop it—the tears just kept coming.

What was making me feel this way? Why now?

After nearly twenty minutes on the floor, I finally mustered up the strength to get to my car and head home. As I put the car into drive, the voice in my head got louder and louder.

When are you going to faint next? What happens if you faint while driving home? What happens if you hit someone, or get in a car crash and die?

I'd driven less than a mile when panic overtook my body again and I became fearful of fainting behind the wheel. I remembered being told, in a doctor's appointment a few weeks prior, that if I ever felt lightheaded or faint to try and get my heart rate up by doing jumping jacks or running. I looked for a place to pull over.

With jeans and a button-up on, I began running wind sprints through University Park on Willamette to try and shake these feelings. If I could get my heart rate up high enough, I might be able to make the fifteen-minute drive from North Portland to my downtown apartment.

Back and forth I ran until my heart was pumping as fast as it could. I hurried to the car and made it only one mile driving until the panic hit again and I had to pull over and collect my thoughts, trying my best to convince the voice in my head that I'd be OK.

I'd been driving for over a decade and always felt confident behind the wheel. Why could I now not even make it a mile?

Finding the courage to keep going, I rolled the windows down and blasted Coldplay on level ten and focused on my breathing. Gripping the wheel as tightly as I could, staying laser focused on the lanes and my breathing, I made it to my parking spot at The Civic. I trekked up to my apartment above the Portland Gear store where I collapsed on the couch and dissolved into tears.

I was exhausted, my body drained, and feeling even more confused as to why this had all just happened.

Little did I know this would become the start of a new chapter in my life on self-awareness and personal development. With the near-overnight growth of Portland Gear and the self-inflicted pressure I began putting on myself in the early days, I was moving faster than my body and mind could keep up with. My body started crying out to be noticed, and in strange ways. It was time to dive in and begin to figure Marcus out.

* * *

In 2013 I began journaling about what I was going through as a human and businessperson. I'd dreamed that one day I'd have a reason to tell my story, and this book is a manifestation of that dream.

This book is a chronological story of every memory through 2019 and how Portland Gear was born. My hope is that it will become Volume 1, and that as my journey continues, I'll have more stories and lessons to share. My reason for putting this

INTRODUCTION

book together is to have something to pass along to my kids, in hopes that they'll be proud of their dad and what he has been able to create. I also have such amazing and wonderful friends and family members whom I promise to give the recognition they deserve.

I love community—it's my binding ingredient—and this book is an inside look at the community Portland Gear has been so fortunate to be part of and build. It's my goal as a storyteller for you to feel part of this story, if you don't already, and for you to find yourself somewhere on these pages as you turn through them.

Portland Gear will always remain a huge part of what I've done, but it does not define who I am. There's more to me than what Portland may know me for, and as I head into a new chapter of life as a father, leader, and teacher, I'm excited to share the layers and complexities that've shaped me over the years.

Since my entrepreneurial journey first began in 2008, I've been on one hell of a ride. Over the coming pages I'll open up about my vulnerabilities, insecurities, shortcomings, and moments of joy. I'm proud of what we've built at Portland Gear and hope you enjoy learning about the inspiration behind the brand, our emphasis on community, and how the P logo was born.

Yes, Portland Gear sells T-shirts and hats, but what we really love selling is the beautiful, complex, and ever-changing community and pride of Portland. This book is meant to celebrate a part of Portland's culture throughout its pages, and I hope you find entertaining and informative stories that make you proud to call this place home or that inspire you to follow your own dreams and find ways to create community where you are.

I am a Product of the People I've surrounded myself with: loving parents; supportive friends; an accepting community; engaging teachers; and a unique, incredible city. I couldn't have created Portland Gear without their influence, and for that, I'm forever grateful. I hope Portland Gear always feels like a Product of the People, a brand that celebrates and represents the Rose City by listening to its community and allowing them to experience Portland in an engaging and inclusive way. That has always been my goal.

CHAPTER 1

FAMILY FIRST

BORN IN 1990 IN PORTLAND, OREGON, TO TWO AMAZING, supportive, hard-working, middle-class parents, I was a nineties kid through and through. I grew up watching Michael Jordan in his prime, Kobe bursting onto the scene, Ken Griffey Jr. with his smooth left-hand swing, Bill Nye the Science Guy on TV; and, of course, playing games on our teal iMac computer with dial-up internet.

My dad, Brian, started in banking right out of college and worked his way up through the insurance and finance industries. My mom, Karen, a third-generation educator, joined the ranks and started teaching in 1981. They met at the University of Oregon in the seventies and later moved to Hillsboro, a suburb of Portland, where they raised my older sister and me.

My dad is a calculated, even-tempered, outdoor loving, kind man. Coming from a hard working family, since the age of fifteen, he worked hard to pay his bills and then to raise our Harvey family of four and save up for my sister's and my college educations. I have countless memories of playing catch in the yard, camping trips, golf outings, and walks with the dog late at night. I love and appreciate my dad very much and can say I'm the person I am today in large part because of him and his character. When I recently asked about his relationship to work, he replied, "I wasn't scared to put my time in the seat; I knew what I needed to do." In other words, he put his self-interest aside to make sure our family was always taken care of. I really appreciate him for that.

My mom is the heartbeat of the family. Born in San Francisco and raised in Chicago, New Jersey, and Portland, she came from a family of laughter and leadership. She has always made sure the people around her are having a good time, are well fed, and feel included in whatever activity she has planned. She taught me the idea of community and how creating moments for other people can bring true joy. I'm incredibly grateful to have absorbed this part of her personality.

My grandma and great-grandma were both schoolteachers, so it was natural for my mom to follow in their footsteps. We were raised to take school seriously and to know the importance of respecting our teachers. Mom knew them all personally from working in the same school district, so there wasn't much wiggle room for messing around. Because of this, my sister and I both always did well in school. The Harvey family was raised on the importance of education and family, and I look forward to passing that along to my kids one day as well.

My sister, Kayla, laid the foundation for me. Since she was five years older, we never went to the same school at the same time, but this didn't mean all the teachers weren't ready for me when my time came. Kayla set the bar high, and there was a similar expectation on me to be a good kid and student. She has believed in me and my crazy business ideas from the beginning, and I'm forever in debt to her for that belief and support. I lived with her for a while after college, so she was the one who had to put up with my late-night idea sessions explaining a new concept I was working on or something I'd read about and wanted to try. She'd patiently listen, nod, and encourage me to do whatever it was I felt compelled to do. Thanks, Kay.

My sister married Jonny, and together they have two wonderful kids, Ashton and Wesley, who I so fortunately get to be a funcle (fun uncle) to. When Ashton walks into my office, his little face lights up at all the "things" I have around, and I'm always sure to send him home with something special. I'll be ready when they need their first summer jobs, too.

Even when my family was unsure of what I was working on or what business idea I'd have next, they were always supportive and allowed for me to just be me. They gave me space to enjoy the things I did and wanted to see me succeed in anything I chose. I look back now and realize the importance of such a close support system that allowed me to dream big and try things. For that, I'm eternally grateful.

As Portland Gear has gotten bigger and I have gotten busier over the years, my mom now says, "We just have to Google you to keep up now." It makes me laugh and feel proud at the same time.

* * *

My childhood revolved around the Oregon Ducks, Nike, and sports. If we weren't at Autzen Stadium or the Rose Garden for a game, we'd be huddled around the TV at home, all yelling at the refs anxiously as the clock ticked down. If a Duck football game was too close, Mom would often disappear upstairs, not to be seen until the next morning, because she couldn't watch.

Some of our best family memories were loading up the station wagon and heading down I-5 south to Eugene for Oregon Duck football games.

Once a year we'd stay at the Phoenix Inn hotel before a game, where I'd swim in the pool all night and eat the free continental breakfast the next morning—my favorite! With eye black under my eyes and the latest Nike Duck jersey on, I'd make my family arrive at games early and stay late so I could try and collect autographs, a glove, or—better yet—a used sweaty wristband or towel.

When it wasn't football season, you'd find me rooting for the Portland Trail Blazers.

For photos taken on my second birthday, my parents put me in a Blazer jersey and fresh Nikes and gave me a basketball; it's as if they were predicting my future. You can still find this image on the family staircase wall, which always makes for a good laugh when friends come over.

I've truly been a Duck and Blazer fan since birth.

Going to the Rose Garden with my dad for the first time was amazing—I was mesmerized! I couldn't believe how tall and athletic the players were. I'd always dreamed of dunking a basketball and playing in the NBA, and I was tiny at the time, so seeing these guys in person was jaw-dropping. I loved the game of basketball, but the shoes, jerseys, wristbands, and warm-ups were almost more important to me than the game itself. There was just something special about the gear the players used that I found so fascinating and still do to this day!

As much as I was into the Ducks and Blazers, there was one thing that beat them both: my love for Nike. Growing up, I was ten minutes away from the Nike World Headquarters in Beaverton and passed it on the way to my grandma's house every week. Nike HQ was my Disneyland, my happiest place on Earth.

Nike was created on the track at the University of Oregon by Bill Bowerman and Phil Knight, and you can feel its presence as you walk around campus. Phil was born and raised in Portland and went to the University of Oregon, which made me feel like I could follow him and start something big one day, too. Being a proud Duck, he always made sure the University of Oregon had the latest and greatest jerseys and gear, and from a young age, I wanted to wear and have it all.

Growing up, the Nike logo, T-shirts, colors, designs, and sponsored athletes were some of my favorite things in the world, and I dreamed of working on campus one day. Every so often on the way to Grandma's house I'd convince my parents to pull off the road so I could sneak onto campus and manifest my future.

The lake in the middle of campus was known for having hundreds of Canadian geese that called it home. I remembered telling my parents, "I'd even pick up goose poop if it meant I could work here one day. I want one of those black Nike badges with my name on it so bad!"

Nike began controlling my every thought and shaping the person I was becoming.

I'd run from window to window, peeking through the glass for a chance to see a sample shoe or unreleased gear. In one, I saw a wall full of fabric swatches and printed color cards hanging from pins, and in another, a rack of unreleased Nike shoes and balls. Because of what I saw, I felt like I was part of an exclusive club—Club Nike—and now I had information only employees were able to have. Behind those walls were things that one day the entire world would see, and I wanted to someday be the one making them.

A mile from the headquarters is a hidden warehouse called the Nike Employee Store, open exclusively to employees and friends who can shop for 40 percent off. I tried many times to convince my mom to give up her thirty-year teaching career to work in the daycare on campus so I could have access to the Nike Employee store, but it never worked. She did, however, have a student teacher at the time whose husband worked at Nike, and every so often we'd get passes from him to go in.

For days leading up to it, knowing I was getting in, I wouldn't sleep. When I walked through those doors, I felt like I was in Willy Wonka's Chocolate Factory. From rack to rack I'd run as fast as I could, seeing all the new products. If any of the new Michael Jordan shoes were there, I'd beg my parents to let me buy them.

I'd run through the warehouse for as long as my parents would let me, literally smelling new shoe boxes and seeing if anyone famous was walking around. Whatever my parents would let me buy would become my prized possessions, and I'd obsess about them for weeks.

As a twelve-year-old kid, little did I know that working at the Nike Employee Store would become my first-ever job and lay the foundation for my love of retail and product.

* * *

Thanks to our local high school basketball coach, I was able to get into a Nike Summer Basketball Camp on campus, reserved exclusively for kids of employees. It was held in the Bo Jackson building, where I'd seen a photo of Michael Jordan playing on the very court I was playing on. Me, little Marcus, would get to do a basketball camp at the Nike Campus, and on the same floor where Michael Jordan walked; I thought I might have died and gone to heaven.

After camp each night I'd go home, scrub my shoes until they were spotless, rearrange my Michael Jordan basketball cards for the hundredth time, and get ready for the next day of camp—fourteen hours early.

The Oregon Ducks, Blazers, and Nike were foundations of my childhood, and I owe a lot to how they shaped my thoughts and desires for the world. That campus made me feel like I had a purpose and was capable of doing something big with my life, something that mattered. The thought that the creator of Nike was born in Portland and went to the University of Oregon just like I'd later do was always encouraging. I had the spirit of Nike in my veins and wanted to be known as a disrupter just like he was.

LIFE LESSONS LEARNED

- → Experience new things, often.
- → Love the things you love.
- → Have big dreams, even if they may seem weird.
- → Where you're going is heavily influenced by where you've been.
- → Go Ducks!

CHAPTER 2

THE CLAWSET

AT THE AGE OF SEVENTEEN, I BEGAN RUNNING MY FIRST business: the student store. During my junior year at Century High School, I decided to focus on business and marketing, knowing it would help me land my dream job at Nike. I enjoyed school, never skipped class, did my homework, and got good grades, but being around my friends is what made me tick and feel alive. You could find me in the front row at every football game, leading the cheers and making sure students showed up to support our athletes. If I wasn't at Sonic with a car full of friends for half-off slushies, I was with my buddies playing sports at the park. I was always on the go.

I felt the most confident and like myself when surrounded by my peers.

Heading into my senior year, I had to pick a year-long project for my marketing class. My favorite teacher, Mr. Bunting, was young and relatable, and he enjoyed teaching about business, marketing, advertising, and entrepreneurship. I knew if I worked hard in his classes, he might bestow upon me the most coveted senior project of them all—running the student store called "The Clawset."

After a few gentle nudges reminding him of my desire to run the store, he handed me a three-ring binder outlining my job responsibilities and the keys to the shop. "We'll see you in the fall," he said. "The project is yours."

The student manager of The Clawset was responsible for controlling the overall retail environment; marketing the store; hiring employees; ordering all the drinks, candy, chips, and pizza; depositing cash; and special projects.

I'd come to love the idea of retail—helping customers, providing service, and ensuring they enjoyed their experience. Working at Nike the summer before, I had the chance to help big-name athletes and celebrities when they'd shop, so I figured my peers would be easy. I was excited to take on The Clawset and build out a similar experience.

Tuesday mornings were for ordering from Coca-Cola, and Thursdays from Frito Lay. I ordered Panera bagels every morning and Pizza Schmizza once a week. Such nutritious food to be feeding students, right?

At 8 a.m., before school, I'd roll up the gate to the store, turn on pop top hits on my Microsoft Zune, and create a fun place for students and friends to come hang out. I'd sell more bags of candy and chips in one lunch than the whole school cafeteria would sell in a week. Every day, The Clawset's sales ranged from $500–$1,000, which I'd log and deposit with the school clerk.

For basketball season, my binder of responsibilities said I had to design, print, and sell a "Keller Krew" T-shirt. Scott Keller was our men's basketball coach at the time, and our student section was called the Krew. I was to call Frye's Athletics in Forest Grove to do the printing, as they were the vendor of choice for the school.

"Hello—can I help you?" said a kind voice on the other end of the phone.

"Hi—yes—my name is Marcus Harvey, from Century High School, and I was told to call you about printing this year's student shirts."

"Great! We'll be happy to help. Do you have the artwork ready in an .ai file?"

"To be honest, I have no clue what that means; this is my first time doing this," I replied helplessly.

"It's a particular type of art that's used for screen printing, so the shirts have crisp lines."

"Sounds cool! Once I can figure out the .ai file, what else will you need from me?"

"Do you know what kind of blank T-shirt you'll be using?" she asked.

"What kind of blank T-shirt... Hmm. Truthfully, I didn't even know there were different types."

"Yes," she said, chuckling on the other end. "We have 100 percent cotton and cotton-poly blends. We have T-shirts that are cheaper in quality and some that are more expensive. We can get you anything!"

At this point, my mind was overwhelmed, and I just needed to get these ordered, so I told her the cheapest one would be fine. The Gildan 2000 it was.

"Great! Now, what color?"

What color? I didn't even know what the shirt was going to look like!

"We'll do black," I said.

"Now, what color ink?"

At this point, it was almost comical to me how many parts there were to a simple T-shirt; I just needed to order them!

"Well, what color inks do you have?" I asked, tossing the question into the wind, hoping she could help me find a direction.

"We can match any Pantone color, but we also have some special inks, like neon, reflective, and glitter."

"Since I have no clue what Pantone means, let's go with something crazy like reflective. Thanks!" I replied.

As the conversation came to a close, I was left to figure out the most important part: what was I going to put on the shirt?

I am not an artist; if we're being honest, I'm pretty terrible at the traditional forms of art. Give me a pen and paper and I'm worthless; I can't draw or conceptualize anything cool, which is why I gravitated toward marketing instead of design to pursue my Nike dreams. I took art classes in high school but wasn't gifted in that area. I wasn't raised with sketchbooks or an abundance of creativity—I just wanted to shoot hoops and hang out with my friends.

When I saw kids in class design and come up with cool ideas, it frustrated me. I'd think to myself, *How is that even possible? How can someone look at a piece of paper, have something come to them, and be able to translate it to something that looks cool?* The best thing I could draw was a game of hangman, and even that seemed just OK.

I take that back; I was pretty good at drawing those S designs, too—the ones where you draw three lines on top, three lines on the bottom, and then connect them. You know what I'm talking about.

Art was always hard for me; my brain just didn't work in that way. I began asking around in my group of friends if anyone knew Adobe Illustrator, the design software I needed to submit, and luckily, my buddy Tyler said he did.

At the time there was only one computer in the school with Adobe Illustrator installed, so Tyler and I walked to the back of the computer lab and blew off the dust. During our lunch break, we started to design what would become the Keller Krew tee and my first-ever piece. Tyler asked what it should look like, and all I could think of was the Superman logo, but instead of an S, we could change it to a K for Keller. After seeing the design come to life on the screen, I thought it was the coolest shirt ever to grace the Earth. With no revisions or peer review, we sent it off to Frye's and ordered twenty-four black Gildan shirts with reflective ink, costing $4.75 each.

Two weeks later, when the shirts were complete, I drove out in my 2004 Mitsubishi Lancer to pick them up. When I got back to school, I had a few of my best friends meet me at The Clawset to snap a pic. I didn't have a nice camera, so I had someone walking by use my flip phone to take a group photo of us standing together smiling. I made flyers with the picture and "Get your Keller Krew shirt at The Clawset now! Only $5!" typed in a clear bold font and posted them all over the school.

Within minutes of opening the store the next day, all the shirts sold out and there was a line of kids waiting because they didn't get one. They may have sold out because of how cheap they were (and no, a $0.25 profit is not a suitable margin, for all you businesspeople reading this), but I was elated to see the shirts sell and people putting them on. Instantly, kids all over school were wearing my T-shirt and using it as a symbol of community and pride. I loved it.

I wanted people to like this shirt as much as I did and feel part of the Krew, so I began wearing it every day. If people saw me loving and rocking it, maybe it'd make them want to, as well! I felt confident when I was surrounded by people, and this shirt allowed me to create community and fostered that feeling. As I took my position in the heart of the student section at the next home game, I couldn't believe how many people were rocking the T-shirt I had made.

I called Frye's to order more and decided to be bold—I ordered seventy-two shirts this time. If I'd sold twenty-four that fast, maybe seventy-two could sell out in a few weeks. It felt like a big bet, but our school was of a decent size, and basketball season had just started, so I figured I'd take the risk and try to sell more.

When the next batch arrived, they sold out in a matter of days. Although The Clawset wasn't making much money on each sale, I was building community and getting our students excited to root for their home team. This felt like a win.

For one of the home varsity games, the team even wore the shirts for warm-ups on the court! It was an incredible feeling to see an entire student section, the players, and even the parents rocking my Keller Krew tee.

By the end of the season, I'd sold several hundred shirts, which were seen all over Hillsboro for months after.

Having other people believe in what I'd created was life-changing for me as a young entrepreneur. Having others use their hard-earned money to purchase a product that I brought to life changed my perspective on business.

I was beginning to learn the power of community.

LIFE LESSONS LEARNED

→ You'll never get what you don't ask for.
→ Learning new things = growth.
→ Surround yourself with people who have talents you don't.
→ Wear the things you believe in.
→ You're not born with confidence. It's built over time.

CHAPTER 3

A MOTHER'S BELIEF

AFTER HIGH SCHOOL, IT WAS TIME TO FOLLOW MY FAMily's footsteps to the University of Oregon to study business and marketing. While adjusting to this new world, I often found myself making the two-hour drive home on the weekends to see my friends and get a home-cooked meal. You could say I was homesick.

During one visit home, I was in need of a few new outfits and went shopping with my mom. After a few stops at PacSun and Zumiez at the Streets of Tanasbourne in Hillsboro, we ended up at Macy's in the young adult section. I was on the hunt for graphic tees, jeans, and hoodies, but I couldn't find anything I liked or that spoke to my evolving style.

My mom looked me in the eyes and said, "Why don't you just make something yourself?"

Little did she know those words would later change my life.

"I don't know how to design clothes," I replied. "I'm not an artist, either, and was never good in art class."

"What about that shirt you designed last year for Keller Krew as part of your senior project?" she replied.

I shrugged my shoulders, and we headed home empty-handed.

* * *

I didn't make much of this conversation at the time, but my mom's challenge kept popping up in my head once I was back at school.

"Why don't you just make something yourself?"

What did she mean? Did she really think I had the skills to make something cool? I couldn't find clothes that spoke to my style—were there other kids my age having this same problem?

The year was 2009, and skate and surf brands like Billabong, Quicksilver, and Hurley were very popular. I'd never participated in action sports like skateboarding or snowboarding growing up, but I'd always enjoyed the looks of the lifestyle, and I found myself wanting to be a part of it. One of my first jobs in High School was working at the Nike Employee store where I learned about product, how customers relate to what they buy, and what drives them to keep coming back. With the combination of all these interests, I thought I might just be capable of starting my own brand.

I took my mom's challenge to heart and began thinking about

what I could create that would solve the problem I'd experienced in Macy's on that day. I knew I wanted unique graphic tees that were based around a cool brand and at a price point I could afford.

I needed to come up with a brand name, so I started by Googling words that embodied "being different" or "uniqueness" to see if anything would catch my eye.

After writing down several names, words, phrases, and a mixing of letters, I landed on a thesaurus search that prompted a name: Updrift. As I read the definition—"the direction opposite that of prevailing movement of littoral motion"—I knew I had it! That was going to be me! I was going to be the one who did something different and made waves in the industry!

After coming up with the name, it was time to create my first T-shirt. I called the most talented graphic designer friend I had and asked for help. A week later, he sent me the artwork for the first-ever Updrift logo and shirt design, and I nearly fell out of my chair. I thought it was the coolest thing my eyes had ever seen.

Inside the Adobe Illustrator file was an off-white T-shirt template with dark red patterns, shapes, and the new Updrift squiggle logo across the front. I loved the squiggle U-letter logo because it almost looked like the Nike swoosh.

I remembered learning years before that the Nike swoosh logo was made by a local Portland State design student, and I felt like we'd just created the next great one to rival it. I thought my new logo was genius—the U logo spoke to me.

I couldn't afford to make the shirts to sell, so I decided to do pre-orders. I printed the T-shirt mockup next to a grid of lines for name, size, and email, and began walking through the halls of the third-floor, LLC-South dorms in Eugene.

I first went next door where I knew I could sell a T-shirt to my buddy Jesse; and after securing him for a large, it was off to see my new friends, Pat and Miles from southern California, who I thought would like the skate feel. They gladly put down their names and a couple of twenty-dollar bills, and by the end of the day I had pre-sold fifteen shirts and had $300 cash in my pocket.

In 2009, Facebook was starting to gain popularity, and students were on their pages all day long connecting with and messaging people. I figured it would be good to post the new design and brand on my Facebook page to make a few more sales. I knew my parents would buy two, since it was their idea, after all; and after two weeks, I'd sold a total of twenty-four shirts. I called a few printers to shop around for the lowest price and found one outside of Beaverton. Unlike with my first Keller Krew order, this time I knew what to say and sounded like a pro.

"Hi there. I'd like to order twenty-four T-shirts for my new apparel brand, Updrift. I already have the artwork in .ai files and would like to use the Gildan 2000 in an oatmeal color and a dark red ink for the print. I've collected the money in advance and am willing to pay now."

They replied very nicely and said the shirts would cost me $10 each to make and would be completed in two weeks. Knowing I'd charged $20, and sold twenty-four, I would make $240 off that initial order. I'd been bitten by the entrepreneurial bug!

A MOTHER'S BELIEF

Making a profit from something I created and dreamed of instantly changed the way I looked at the world and money. Through hard work and hustle, I'd have the opportunity to make however much money I wanted. There was no limit to what I could do and no one telling me what I was worth. The possibilities were uncapped, and I wanted to see how far I could push myself.

I received the finished shirts two weeks later, hand-delivered them to all my customers with thanks and a smile, and began wearing one every day in hopes of creating more demand for my brand.

I took the initial $240 profit and decided to repeat the process. I called my friend and asked if he'd help me design another shirt, this time something a bit different and more edgy.

With a new design mockup complete and grid paper printed, I took off back down the hall to try and sell round two. This time, however, the sales were more challenging. Everyone who'd bought the first one didn't need another $20 T-shirt two weeks later. I sold a few to people who liked the new design (and didn't buy the first one). I realized I couldn't just keep doing the same thing, so I began thinking of ways to market my product to new people.

Everything I'd read told me good marketing begins with a great story. If I was to make Updrift work, I'd have to start thinking creatively and market in new and innovative ways to get my message out. I needed customers in order to stay afloat, so it was on me to go and find them. I always loved how Nike made me feel part of whatever campaign or new shoe launch they were promoting, and I wanted to bring people along with my journey, too, allowing them to feel part of my community.

One way I thought of was to learn how to do the graphic design and printing myself so I could be in control of the full process and make more unique products. I needed to stand out in a crowded marketplace and thought that sharing this story with the customers could drive my business. If I had all the equipment, I could promote myself being the one actually creating the gear, letting the customers feel like it was all custom and made just for them.

It was time to start acting like what my business definition was—that which is opposite of prevailing movement. It was time for me to do something big, take the risk, and create for the world what I couldn't find for myself.

LIFE LESSONS LEARNED

→ Allow others to see things you may not see in yourself.
→ Always try new things. It's the only way forward.
→ Naïveté can be your biggest strength.
→ Value the people who support you.
→ Think different. Channel your Updrift.

CHAPTER 4

THE BATHTUB WILL DO

DURING THE SUMMER OF 2009, I USED ALL MY SAVINGS and purchased a four-color screen-printing machine from screenprinting.com. I began watching YouTube videos to better understand the process. I had goals of printing all my own gear and using it to create some extra side money. My starter kit included everything I'd need to launch a printing business, and when it arrived, I began setting it up in my parents' garage.

"Burning screens," as it was called, was the process of getting an image embedded into the screen so it could then be printed onto shirts—and I was terrible at it. To create a screen for printing, I had to evenly coat it with a light-sensitive pink emulsion, place a printout of the image I wanted to print on top, and expose a light from above onto the screen, which would harden every part except where my print was. This whole process had to be done in a dark room, and being at my parents' house still, I converted the upstairs family bathroom into my workshop.

I messed this process up so many times it became comical, and restarting was no simple task! I'd have to walk down the white-carpeted stairs, screen dripping with pink goo, go outside to power-wash the screen clean so I could restart, and then head back upstairs to repeat thirty minutes later. Sometimes it would take all day to make one good screen, and the carpet would end up covered with pink dots from me dripping up and down the stairs. It never bothered my parents as long as I pulled out the OxiClean and cleaned up by the morning. Thanks, Mom and Dad.

The process needed more space and ventilation than a small upstairs bathroom could provide, but that was all I had, so I was forced to make it work. With a finished "burned screen" in hand, I'd head to the garage and place it in my small metal printing machine, pull my first shirt onto the flat surface under the screen, and get ready to print. The kit only came with three colors of ink, so my early shirts were limited, but with every passing of the squeegee across the screen, a new shirt was born.

After a few weeks of trial and error on my Updrift products, I realized I'd need to start selling shirts to help pay off the $1,000 machine. I reached out to businesses and friends, offering my services for screen-printed shirts, and received my first job from a neighbor who owned a local transmission shop and needed sixty orange shirts with his logo on them for an upcoming party.

I ordered the blank shirts as cheaply as I could online and, after a few days of practicing, messing up, and reprinting, and late nights in the garage, I delivered the completed shirts to my neighbor's shop. One week after dropping them off and cashing his check for $600, I received a call from him: "After giving the shirts away at our party, all my customers called and said the white ink washed out in the laundry and the shirts are ruined. We need to fix this."

Shit. I knew I was getting better at making shirts, but this proved I was not ready to sell my products and needed more time to perfect them. I didn't feel confident in my ability to remake the shirts, so I refunded his entire check and ended up losing a few hundred dollars on the project. It was the opposite of what I'd hoped for when I'd taken the job.

Although I barely had enough money to cover the loss, I knew in my core the right thing to do was to give him his money back. Not holding up my end of the deal and being honest about it was more important than the money lost, and I realized in that moment how much I value connection and reputation over revenue and profit.

I was never able to perfect the process of garage screen-printing, and I quickly realized my time was better spent on things I was good at and wanted to improve on. Although I invested a lot of time and money that summer in my failed screen-printing business, it became a learning experience I'm incredibly glad I had. After summer was over and it was time to head back to Eugene, I decided to sell the machine, cut my losses, and put my time elsewhere. Looking back now, I'm so appreciative of that summer, as I feel it really helped lay the foundation for my future success.

* * *

The same summer I was learning screen printing in the garage, I started working on marketing Updrift in a more unique way and selling my "story" better. I began heading to local skateparks with armfuls of gear looking for kids who'd be willing to trade for allowing me to take photos of them. I knew Nike was founded on utilizing athletes and their exposure. I thought I should do the same.

At the Tualatin Hills Skatepark in Beaverton, I asked the skaters who the best rider was, and they all pointed to a young kid who, with headphones dangling from his shirt, went flying by us and landed a big jump off a ramp. They said his name was Smalex. I felt like I was looking at the future global face of Updrift.

I pulled him aside, introduced myself, and asked if he'd take a free shirt in exchange for posing for a few photos. He said yes, and with my dad's borrowed camera, I tried my best to take pictures like I'd seen in the skate magazines. I'd lie on my back under a rail, run alongside him, and even let him jump over me if it just meant I could capture a cool photo of my new Updrift tee.

Next, I brought the family video recorder to the park and tried to make a skate highlight video. I'd never filmed or edited anything before, but I was willing to spend the time to learn if it meant more exposure for my brand. Watching tutorials on YouTube, I learned the signature skate video look was created with a fisheye lens attachment, so I purchased the cheapest one I could find online. After filming over the span of a few afternoons, I sat down to edit the video and noticed every shot had a hair in the video that must have gotten stuck in the lens. I didn't have time or want to refilm it all, so I edited the video and posted it on YouTube anyway.

With two riders on my newly formed Updrift skate team, I decided that entering local skate contests might help spread the word about my brand and give me an opportunity to take more photos of my riders. I knew Smalex was pretty good and would have a chance to win a contest wearing the Updrift logo.

Growing up, being a sports agent had looked fun, and this venture provided an opportunity for me to get to live out that dream. I'd have to drive my skaters around, take care of them, and hope that the exposure they'd give us would be good for the brand and help sell some more tees.

One weekend, I took the guys to a contest in Salem, Oregon, that—oddly enough—my cousin was putting on. I printed a few wild Updrift shirts in the garage, splattered them with paint, picked up the riders, and got on the freeway to head south. Even though I was younger than my oldest rider, I liked the pressure of taking care of them and helping them succeed.

I knew one role of a sports agent and brand manager was to make sure the athletes were always fed and able to perform at their peak ability. I couldn't afford much at the time, so I decided McDonald's would have to do. We all ate for under $10, and the guys were stoked on a free meal and ready to hit the contest!

I registered the guys in their respective age groups, pulled out a rack of shirts from my Mitsubishi Lancer, and set them out for sale. I took photos of the guys competing in their Updrift shirts (which were also for sale if someone saw and wanted one) and tried my best to build buzz and make us look like a bigger deal than we were.

"Updrift is a local skate brand from up in Portland," I'd say over and over to anyone who'd listen, trying my hardest to make a sale. I don't think I sold a single shirt that day. Seeing the Updrift team wearing my gear, seeing the content I was creating, and being able to tell my story made me realize that creating a brand would be really hard, but also worth it. Everything would have to fit perfectly together to create a compelling story and make people want to buy my product, and I just felt like it wasn't there yet. I was willing to do the work and figure it out, but I didn't know the next steps.

Even though I ended up losing money that summer, every day became part of my story. From burning screens, dripping on the carpet, and making bad shirts in the garage to putting myself out there at the skatepark and building a wannabe skate team, it forever changed my life. The summer of 2009 became a massive part of my foundation. It was a time when I wasn't scared to take risks, because I had nothing to lose! I felt a sense of conviction knowing I was onto something, even if what I was trying wasn't always working out.

LIFE LESSONS LEARNED
→ Be curious and bold. It'll lead to something unexpected.
→ Take a risk on yourself.
→ Your reputation is always worth more than money.
→ Failing fast is helpful. It allows you to find what you're good at sooner.
→ Everything is part of your story. Embrace it.

CHAPTER 5

THE T-SHIRT GUY

DURING MY SOPHOMORE YEAR AT THE UNIVERSITY OF Oregon, I began feeling anxious about my selected major, and if I was even going to the right school. The dark, rainy winters made the homesickness worse, and I even considered a move to California to chase some sun. Although I had a 3.8 GPA in high school, I never fully learned how to study, because so much of the grades were participation- and homework-based.

College was a different story.

With grades based solely on a midterm and final, I quickly started to underperform. High school hadn't set me up for how hard college would be, and for the first time in my life, I felt unprepared.

At a welcome BBQ, I was approached by a young gentleman about fraternity life but instantly shot down the idea. Although my mom and sister had been in sororities, I headed to college with an anti-fraternity mindset from the get-go and didn't feel like it was for me. The only things I knew about fraternities were what I'd seen portrayed in the movies and, still looking like a sixteen-year-old, I figured I wouldn't fit in.

After attending an event with Pat and Miles from my hall, I was exposed to something totally unexpected: community. Yes, it was an old, run-down house that had a faint smell of fifty years of beer on the floor, but it felt warm for some reason, and the guys were welcoming. I was told that Delta Tau Delta had won top grades several years running, with the average member carrying a 3.4 GPA. The sophomores and juniors lived in the house, while the seniors would live together in houses close by. As a group, they'd attend social events, go to the basketball and football games, play intramural sports, and study. It felt like a brotherhood, and as a young, impressionable, community-oriented person, I wanted to be included.

I joined that fall and instantly found a group of friends I'd begin to grow with. I felt safe surrounded by these people, and it made school more enjoyable right away.

During a formal fraternity dinner in the spring, one of the senior members showed us an interactive art exhibit he'd created as part of his digital art major. Although I'd never considered myself an artist before, the project intrigued me, and I began asking him questions about the program and what classes were like.

"Class is fun and challenging, and you get to make things and see them come to life," he said.

I'd been wanting to learn Adobe Illustrator and Photoshop

since I'd been utilizing them for Updrift, and when I saw that the intro-level classes taught the basics, I signed up. Having to always ask people to help me with designs was frustrating, so learning the tools and being able to do it myself seemed beneficial.

A week into my first digital arts class, I was hooked! The classroom was full of brand-new Apple computers, screen printing machines, vinyl cutters, heat presses, and digital tablets; and the walls were covered with student-created posters, flags, and stickers. I felt like I was working at Nike—it looked just like all those windows at the Nike Headquarters I'd peeked in through as a kid.

I quickly went from getting Bs and Cs on my midterms and finals to now being graded on projects and my own creativity. I felt like I was finally learning something I could easily use in the real world, and I loved it!

I'd never considered myself an artistic person, but after realizing that art wasn't just painting, sculpting, or drawing, my mindset began to change. This new form of digital art was fascinating to me, and I felt I could mix my business mind and the new talents I was acquiring to create something special.

In 2010, a devastating earthquake hit the country of Haiti and I had an opportunity to use my art for good. As a student with a desire to add value to the world, and with my passion for T-shirts, I decided to create and print a shirt to raise money for the natural disaster relief fund. I designed a simple shirt to sell but realized that, to make a more significant impact, I needed the help of a larger organization to spread my message.

Through a fraternity friend, I was put in contact with the University of Oregon Bookstore buyer, who told me they'd love to help. In order to be sold at the bookstore, the shirts would have to go through the store's preferred screen-printing company, McKenzie Sew-On, and I was to reach out to their rep, Joel.

After explaining the process of working with McKenzie Sew-On and getting me set up, Joel invited me into their shop for a tour. When I walked in, I knew I was looking at my future. The back of the warehouse was large and cranking out shirts for the Ducks, Nike, Ninkasi Brewing, and Dutch Brothers—a fast-growing coffee company out of southern Oregon.

Later that day, I posted about the shirts on my Facebook page and shared the link with my fraternity members. The community really got behind my project and started supporting it in big ways right off the bat. Before I knew it, there was a section of shirts right as you walked into the main bookstore, and people all over campus began wearing my shirt and posting about the cause on their Facebook pages. It got so big that the Oregon women's basketball team wore the shirts for warm-ups before a game, getting me front-page exposure in the campus newspaper.

Seeing the ladies wear those shirts on the floor brought me right back to my Keller Krew days in high school where I had seen the whole student body and the team wearing my design for the first time. With these latest shirts, we ended up raising thousands of dollars for the relief fund, but the connection to McKenzie Sew-On would end up having a much-larger-than-anticipated impact on my life.

* * *

Did you know that nearly 80 percent of college students end up changing their major at least one time? I always thought I'd be the one to defy those odds, land the dream job at Nike in sports marketing right after school, and be on my way. But God had a different plan. After taking a few more digital arts classes, I had the talk with my parents about changing my major and pursuing something I was extremely interested in, and they supported me right away. With Updrift still taking up all my free time and becoming a true passion project, my parents could see how interested I was and how, when I talked about it, I'd light up with excitement.

In class, I began learning more about color, font, layout, and branding, and how the design applications and tools worked. Not only was I able to take graphic design classes, but I also gained skills in web design, photography, stop-motion, video, and more.

I truly wanted to get better for my own sake, so I spent my nights and weekends trying out new techniques and designing logos, T-shirt graphics, and stickers. It didn't come easily to me; but having cool teachers I wanted to learn from and other students in my program who were motivating me to be better were a huge help.

I saw myself learning skills I wanted to get better at and use for a long time. I wanted to go to class, stay up late working on projects, and share my creations. I saw how the things I designed and the products I created made people feel, and I loved making those connections. To see something go from a little idea in my head to a screen, then onto a sticker, T-shirt, or poster, made me begin looking at art in a different way.

***

Part of my senior project was to find an internship for the spring term that related to things we were learning. As most students began applying for open positions at local ad agencies or big businesses, I reached back out to Joel at McKenzie Sew-On and pitched him on what I was willing to do with the skills I was acquiring.

"I will help with the art department, fold shirts, pack orders, clean the warehouse—whatever is needed," I said.

I'd like to think Joel's answer had something to do with my resilience and desire to be part of their team—but once I added that I would do it unpaid, he said yes.

There was no internship posting I applied for or person who helped connect me; I simply reached out to the place I wanted to give my time to and learn from, and I put an offer on the table they couldn't resist. Someone was always going to have a better GPA than me or a stronger résumé, but no one was going to out-network or out-work me when it came to something I wanted.

The next few months were incredible as I continued to hone my skills in apparel, graphic design, and the business side of screen printing. I asked Joel if I brought the company new clients, would he pay me a commission? Or, better yet, let me print my Updrift product for free? He said yes again, and as I began going around campus selling jobs to fraternities, groups, churches, and friends, I racked up a pretty good tab to cover the costs to print my own product. My next run of Updrift shirts would cost $0, and I'd sell them for $20 each, thus creating 100 percent profit to reinvest and make more!

I quickly began to build a reputation for myself around campus as "The T-shirt Guy"—which, for a single, twenty-year-old college kid maybe wasn't the sexiest title, but at least people were starting to remember me.

In addition to the internship, I was required to complete a senior project in my art class. Like The Clawset in high school, I decided to build out and run a small retail store for Updrift. I made signs and wall graphics, designed and printed new shirts, made cool boxes and lookbooks, and curated a corner of the building to call my own over the weekends. The entire process was so fun, and I felt like I was working in a real role at a real company. A lot of things I loved in life were beginning to come together, and I saw how the more I combined my interests, the more I loved what I was doing.

Growing up, I'd had my fair share of insecurities, but as I began feeling more and more confident in my design abilities and what I was creating, I noticed they started going away. These new skills I was acquiring felt like something I could actually control, and that began giving me a new mindset on life.

I realized all these qualities in myself I'd seen as negative were becoming what made me unique and memorable. This whole confidence thing was new to me, but the more T-shirts I created, people I talked to, events I was part of, and connections I made, the better I felt about myself. I didn't run from my insecurities; I pushed through them and put the energy I had previously wasted thinking about them toward something I could control.

From creating the coolest fraternity T-shirts on campus all four years, to seeing a shirt I designed in the Oregon Duck Bookstore, to having my digital arts senior project be a pop-up Updrift store, the final years of college were truly transformative. I'd built a supportive community of friends, professors, and fraternity brothers, and I felt confident in my abilities to create designs that brought them all together. By following a passion, I was able to combine my love for business with these newly-acquired design skills to create someone I was proud to be.

I never took an entrepreneurship or finance class in school, and since Day One of operating my businesses, I always just did what felt right. I never felt confined to doing things "the usual way" and gave myself the freedom to carve out my own path. I was beginning to trust my gut and have confidence in my decisions. I wanted to be unique, I wanted to be me, and I began realizing that the more I did things my way, the more satisfied I was. Some could even say I was moving in "the direction opposite that of prevailing movement of littoral motion." I was becoming the definition of Updrift.

LIFE LESSONS LEARNED

- → Find community wherever you are. It'll make life more fun.
- → Pay attention to the room. You never know what you can learn.
- → Have integrity and do what's right, even when things aren't going your way.
- → Find confidence in what you're good at and do those things more.
- → Only worry about things you can actually control.

CHAPTER 6

FIRED

AFTER GRADUATING FROM THE UNIVERSITY OF OREGON, I packed three boxes of Updrift tees and one bag of clothes and hit the road to California. I'd always wanted to take a solo road trip, and that summer felt like perfect timing. I wanted to put off getting a "real" job a bit longer, and with fraternity brothers and family members throughout California, I'd have plenty of free places to stay. Over the next thirty days, I explored over fifteen cities and was on the lookout for inspiration. One night I'd be exploring LA and crashing on my cousin's couch, and the next I'd be in a beautiful guest house in San Clemente exploring the sun-soaked beaches.

I never had anywhere to be and had the ultimate freedom to roam cities, stumble into retail stores, explore backroads, and learn more about myself. I'd chat with business owners, local artists, musicians, or anyone else who had a few minutes and wanted to share their story. I became a listener.

Los Angeles has an incredible apparel district, so I spent days walking streets, peeking into shops and looking for factories that I might one day be able to work with. I'd always loved apparel but never fully understood how it was made, so this trip allowed me the flexibility to search for these answers. I wanted to learn more about the process; it became an obsession.

While in San Diego, I stumbled upon a local skatepark and started chatting with the kids there. They said there was a skate contest the next day, and I asked if anyone wanted to wear a free Updrift shirt while competing. Several of the kids were thrilled with this opportunity and said yes, which allowed me a chance to get some cool new photos for my Facebook page.

The following morning, one of the kids who'd said yes ended up winning third place, and I saw an Updrift shirt on a podium for the first time.

Living on the road was fun. I found inspiration around every corner and loved the warm beaches where I'd people-watch and hang out for hours on end. As I started running out of money, I felt Oregon was calling me back, and I knew it was time to make the sixteen-hour drive north to settle down.

* * *

My parents worked hard to pay for my college degree, so I felt the pressure to make them proud by getting a job. A majority of my friends and community were still living in Eugene after college, so the idea of staying there a bit longer felt comfortable.

I called Joel at McKenzie Sew-On, where I'd interned, but they didn't have any paid positions, so I was forced to call around town. After weeks of back and forth with the competing print shop, I was offered a job doing inside and outside sales for $12 an hour plus the potential for commission.

If you've spent much time in Oregon, you know how dark and wet the winters can get. Although I was trying my best to learn this new company's systems and assimilate into their culture, my heart was never in it—I didn't like the box I was being put in. I had so many fresh ideas for how to make the company feel younger, change up its marketing, and acquire new clients; but every new suggestion was met with roadblocks. The employees had all been there for years and to me felt very stuck in their ways. None were open to change, which made it hard for an idea man like me to fit in.

I tried bringing in small local brands, University of Oregon athletes, and young clients to do fun and edgy projects, but I was constantly met with attitude and the suggestion that I was being disrespectful. It seemed they had no clue that my ideas were meant to help the entire business—not just me.

Most days, I'd sit patiently at my desk, staring out the window into the rain, waiting for the phone to ring with an order and dreading the possibility that if it didn't, I'd have to start cold-calling around town. I'd catch myself thinking that even if I became a "someone" in Eugene, I'd still be a "nobody" in Portland. I didn't want to become a nobody.

During the annual Thanksgiving company party, the main topic of conversation quickly became, "Let's make fun of Marcus and everything he's doing wrong." When I left that night, I felt down and disappointed. I knew in my core I wasn't supposed to work at a place that didn't value my creative, outside-the-box thinking, but I wasn't sure what to do next.

At 4:37 p.m. on December 15, 2012, that answer came to me, and I experienced a life-altering moment. As I was sitting at my desk in the front reception area, the owner walked to the printer like he did ten times a day—only this time, he turned around, handed me a check, and said, "It's just not working. We're going to let you go."

Shit. What am I going to tell my parents?

I'd just told them I got a job and signed a six-month lease, and I'd heard excitement in their voices when I shared that my major would be put to good use! Ever since high school, teachers and people in my friend group had thought I'd be the one to do something big with my life; and here I was, fired after two months in my first job. I was in shock.

As I walked to my car in the pouring rain, wet check in hand, I was pissed, and my emotions were getting the best of me.

"Screw those guys," I thought to myself. "They don't even know how to run a cool and fun business!"

I went home to my lightly furnished apartment, loaded up my car, and made my way back to Portland. During the two-hour drive, I began calling people I looked up to for advice. First up was an older alumnus from my fraternity whom I'd built a relationship with over the previous few years. He said, "They don't know what they're missing. It's their loss. You're capable of something more than Eugene can give you."

I didn't understand exactly what he meant, so I called my former Nike boss. He said, "Good! Now do something bigger with your life. This is your chance!"

What were they trying to tell me? Did they see something in me I hadn't ever seen in myself?

Finally, I called my sister. "Please don't tell Mom and Dad yet, but I got fired. Can I stay with you tonight?"

She said yes.

* * *

As I hit Salem an hour in, my mind was racing in a million directions. What had I done wrong? Why would they fire me so quickly? Was I really *that* bad?

I was confused, angry, and emotional, but the words of encouragement from those phone calls had me thinking something good could come from losing this job.

Those thoughts I'd been having the month before about wanting out of Eugene... Was being fired today God telling me something? Did I have some sort of destiny to fulfill?

Driving I-5 alone in the pouring rain, I told myself I'd never work for anyone again. Never could someone fire me randomly at 4:37 p.m. or try to put me and my skills in a box. I was willing to do anything to avoid a repeat of that moment. It was time for me to start my journey to becoming my own boss and an entrepreneur.

Waking up at Kayla's house the next day, I knew I'd eventually have to face my fear and tell my parents. The next night, while leaving a family gathering at my grandma's, I quickly said under my breath, "Mom, I was let go from my job already. I guess it was something about reorganizing and downsizing. I'm bummed, but I'll be all right."

Sure, maybe I didn't tell her the full truth. It was embarrassing at the time, and I didn't want to disappoint my parents with the real news that their son had been fired. If I could just buy some time to start something else and make them proud, maybe it would all sort itself out.

"I asked Kayla if I could move in with her for a bit, and she said yes. I mean, it looks like we'll all be spending more time together for the holidays! That's a plus, right?"

LIFE LESSONS LEARNED

- → Always be curious and search for answers.
- → Trust your gut. Sometimes it's all you've got.
- → Own your mess-ups; just get through and move forward.
- → Utilize people in your life you trust. Just make sure to repay them someday.
- → Find your lesson in every situation.

CHAPTER 7

SUCCESSFUL FAILURES

THE COMEDOWN FROM COLLEGE WAS REAL. AFTER moving in with my sister, I began feeling sad that my Eugene years had come to an end. I loved my time there and was so appreciative of the friendships, memories, and lifelong connections I'd made. This new "adulting" thing was hard.

The University of Oregon was where I'd found myself, and it had become my second home. I learned about responsibility, service, kindness, community living, teamwork, and leadership. The memories and connections I made over those four years would later become some of my most cherished in life.

With school done, I had to take learning into my own hands. I started reading business books religiously. I'd go to the Hillsboro Public Library and borrow every business book I could get my hands on and instantly dive in. From *Small Business Taxes for Dummies* and *Start with Why* to *The 4-Hour Workweek*, I began spending every free second reading books and trying to learn something new. I wasn't a reader growing up, but now, wanting to be successful in life and business, I knew it was a trait I'd need to develop.

While sitting alone in my sister's spare room, I made a vision board of all the things I wanted to achieve in my life. I cut out clippings of nice houses, cars, vacation destinations, and celebrities, and I hung it smack-dab in front of my bed where I'd stare at it every morning and night. I'd think about my future, what I wanted it to look like, where I'd live, who I'd marry, and what my job would be.

Every morning, I'd drive four minutes to Starbucks and pretend it was my office. I never bought anything because (1) I didn't have any money, and (2) I don't drink coffee; but it quickly helped me establish discipline and a routine. I knew if I wanted to become successful and not have a boss, I'd have to hold myself to extremely high standards.

I began posting ads on Craigslist every morning offering to help potential clients with their graphic and web design needs. Even though I wasn't very good at these things yet, I had a passion for getting better and knew if someone would pay me to make their product or idea look great, I was willing to put in the time to learn the skills to make it happen.

After a few days of posting with the headline "Cheap web designer for hire!" I got my first inquiry. The lady who reached out owned a consulting company and was looking for a revamp of her website and logo; she asked what I charged.

Only a few short weeks before this I was making minimum wage, but something inside told me to aim high and throw out a ridiculous number to see if she'd bite. I was broke, living at my sister's house, and unemployed. I had nothing to lose by trying.

I replied and told her I'd love to do her project, but I'd charge $90 an hour.

Ninety. Dollars. An. Hour.

I couldn't believe I'd typed that. I figured worst case, she'd say no; second-best case, she'd come back with a counteroffer; and never did I even think there was a chance at best-case, in which she'd just say yes.

Her reply was, "Sounds good! Let's do it!"

JOURNAL ENTRY: 2013

> I emailed her and said my price was $90 an hour. I'm not entirely sure where that number came from, but I aimed high just to see what she'd say, and she said yes!! I can't believe it right now, I'm about to get paid $90 an hour when just a few months ago I was making $12 an hour and hating my job. I'm blown away right now, I feel like my self-worth just went through the roof! I'm going to make nearly eight times what I was and only have to spend eight-tenths the amount of time to complete it. I'm going to get good at doing these.

Just like that, those five little words changed my life. To have someone believe in me more than I believed in myself was so validating. I didn't think I was worth $90 an hour. Heck, I was just recently making minimum wage, remember, and I'd never actually designed for a custom website before.

I didn't want to let her down, so I began working around the clock to make sure she was satisfied. After reading tutorials, watching YouTube videos, and lots of trial and error, I sent her an invoice for $1,600 for the completed project, to which she replied, "Swing by and pick up the check! Looks great!"

I couldn't believe that by merely putting things out into the universe, people would notice and need me. Suddenly I was worth $90 an hour and felt like I could go out and do anything. My mindset did a full one-eighty. I was now walking a bit taller, more confident in my daily Craigslist ads, and beginning to believe in myself as an entrepreneur.

I still had a few screen-printing clients from college I was printing for and needed to find a new, local shop that could help me out. I began by Googling and cold-calling as many spots as I could to ask for "contract pricing" so I could mark it up to clients and make a little bit off the margin. Since I was out doing the sales for them, they'd pass along those savings to me, and I could make money from brokering the deal.

I came across a small shop in Beaverton called H & S Printing and decided to swing by unannounced. Standing behind a puff of dryer smoke was a smiling and inviting face welcoming me in. He introduced himself as Hussein, and we instantly hit it off over our love for Nike and shoes. I told him a bit about myself and how I was looking for a local printer for my client's jobs. He shared his story—coming to America as an Iraqi refugee, putting himself through Portland State, and starting his first print shop in his basement. He kindly gave me a pricing sheet and said he'd look forward to working with me.

The next day I attended my first, and last, networking event. I needed more clients and thought joining a group could be beneficial. As everyone went around the room and shared what they did for work, I proudly stood up and said, "I do freelance apparel design, screen printing, web design, and can help with your social media needs."

Crickets and blank stares followed.

I felt so out of place with most of these people in their fifties selling insurance, real estate, and consulting services that I just quietly sat down and counted the seconds on the clock until the event was over.

The year was 2013 and people hadn't quite figured out what social media was or the power it would wield. I was on Facebook, Twitter, and this new app called Instagram every day and had quickly grown to enjoy and understand them. I liked that they were all a combination of photography, community, and connection. I could tell that they'd be something big. This networking group just didn't care for it. I felt so out of place.

On my way home, I stopped by Hussein's print shop to vent about the event and how it had made me feel.

"I went looking for new people to network with, but no one understood me or what I was trying to do. They just stared at me. I didn't like that vibe," I shared with him.

"Well, why don't you start your own group of people that think the same way as you?" Hussein replied.

It reminded me of when my mom encouraged me to "just make something," and that same feeling came over my body.

"Maybe I should."

After walking out of Hussein's shop that day, I didn't make it two blocks before having to sit and write down all the thoughts that were coming to me.

My brain was firing on all cylinders, and I started piecing together the possible solution and takeaways from that day.

- → Communities are better when people come together and gather.
- → Surround yourself with like-minded people.
- → Specialization is key.
- → Sometimes age does matter.
- → 7 a.m. is too early.

It all made me realize how badly I missed my community in Eugene. I had a few friends and peers back in Portland, but this experience pushed me to set out to create a new name for myself and build a new community.

After a few rounds of name ideas in my head, I landed on "Creative 35." My initial thought was a group of thirty-five design-specific entrepreneurs under the age of thirty-five, thus fixing both of my frustrations from the other networking event. I shared the idea with Hussein, and he was in. He would become my first member, and "screen printer" was now off the list of available roles.

Then I called my old college design friends, and before I knew it, I had a photographer, videographer, and designer on the team. Mack, one of my friends from high school, and a guy named Wookie, whom I'd met in passing at Hussein's shop and knew did full custom apparel design, said they were down to swing by if I ever hosted a get-together.

I wanted to bring all these people together in the same place to see the magic we could create, but the problem was we didn't have a space to meet in. I began calling around town and found a location called The Rose Lounge that offered their space for free, since it would be before opening hours and we'd most likely stay for drinks after.

With twenty people in attendance, I introduced my concept of how we could work together to help each other's businesses and utilize our unique talents to build each other up. Everyone was young, hungry, and looking for community, and you could tell in that first meeting that connections were already being made.

After a few hours of meeting and then staying after for drinks, I remember walking around downtown late that night with Mack and a few other members, talking: "This is going to change Portland and put us on the map. We're going to help shape this city." Maybe it was the cheap vodka and soda, maybe it was my youthful ambition—but staring at the iconic Portland Oregon sign that night, there was just a feeling in my body that in that moment, I was exactly where I was supposed to be.

I created and started a new event called "Fashion Friday" at the Rose Lounge where our group would invite two up-and-coming clothing brands in for a dueling fashion show. I hired a DJ, made sure we all invited everyone we knew, and often jumped on the mic to make sure everyone was having a good time and felt taken care of. Our videographer team member would film (you can still find these videos on YouTube if you want a good laugh), and our photographer would snap group shots that I'd then post to the Creative 35 Facebook page the next day in hopes that people would share and want to attend the following month. I figured if we took good pictures of people, which everyone wants, and put our logo in the corners, the reposted photos would get us new eyeballs and maybe some new followers.

> **JOURNAL ENTRY: 2013**
>
> We shot great photos, put our logo watermarked on and just posted all over Facebook. I hope they can generate some buzz. Team member Jordan made a cool video which got around one hundred views in two days, pretty excited about that. Two weeks later we did it again but wanted to add more substance to it. With all of us being pretty into the fashion and streetwear industry, I came up with a "Battle of the Brands." The idea was each week two brands would go head to head, and the winner would advance to the finals where we could crown a champion. If I could get several brands involved, the goal was for them to help bring more people because I made my money on the door and at the bar. The first two brands were Jaefields and The Incorporated. It was a fun night, that got pretty busy at the end because each brand had their people come out and support. I wanted the brands who can bring the most people and spend the most money so we could keep these events going. I was in charge of the contest on the mic and had everyone pretty engaged and into it. When I posted the gallery on our Facebook page, it said the reach was 2,278 people. That's pretty damn good for us and our second event.

If there was a fashion show or party going on in town, I'd text the group and make sure we'd all roll up together to be seen. One time I bought us front row seats at Portland Fashion Week just so we could get our picture taken and look important.

If this group was to continue, I'd need to start figuring out how we could make a steadier stream of income. With Wookie and I spending the most time together on it, it seemed like doing custom apparel designs and website creation would be our easiest path. It was time to start selling.

LIFE LESSONS LEARNED

- → Aim high when trying to figure out what you're worth.
- → Always bet on yourself.
- → Read lots and lots of books. They'll help expand your mind.
- → Create your own community.
- → If you want to change something about the world, do it.

CHAPTER 8

CAN I STAY A BIT LONGER?

AS THE GROUP BEGAN TAKING SHAPE, WOOKIE, ONE OF OUR members, quickly rose to the top. He was dependable, kind, and loyal—everything I'd need in a business partner. He started his own cut-and-sew menswear brand called Jaefields and was working hard to make it known in Portland. Everything he did was custom, thoughtful, and had an elevated feel to it, something very different from the traditional screen print business model I was used to.

At a coffee shop one morning, Wookie and I began talking about our talents and how we could better utilize them to expand together. We agreed that our passions aligned in menswear apparel, brand building, and design, so we started exploring more what this could all look like as a business.

I loved the storytelling, branding, marketing, finance, and business sides of apparel design, while Wookie enjoyed the creation, development, and design process.

The Fashion Friday parties were fun, and we were slowly getting screen-printing projects and random website clients, but something still just felt incomplete. Sitting in Ava Roasteria that morning, we decided to narrow our focus and make Creative 35 a Custom Apparel Creation Group.

It would be my job to find the clients, build relationships, oversee finance, and handle the screen-printing jobs and project management. Wookie would design the patterns for brands, athletes, and celebrities; source the materials; and get the items sewn by local seamstresses.

The moment we narrowed our focus, it was as if the clouds parted and business started flowing in. Our mission became simple, and the more we shared it with our network, the more opportunities began to come our way.

I'd been living with my sister and her fiancé, Jonny, for several months; they were about to get married in the summer of 2013, so I knew my time with them was coming to an end. Even though I was hustling hard, I wasn't making much money, and I can remember having as little as $17 in the bank. I couldn't afford much, but I began looking at options on Craigslist for cheap apartments in downtown Portland. The first place listed wasn't an apartment, but rather a shared creative office space that looked like something out of the future.

The ad said I could rent a desk in a "co-working space" for $500 a month that was promising to have lots of other creative community members involved.

I was instantly torn.

I knew I needed to move out and start living on my own, but something about this just felt like the next step I needed to take for my business. My heart told me to get an apartment and start growing up, but my gut told me otherwise. I was tired of working from the corner table at Starbucks every day, where I'd leave smelling like burnt coffee, and I wanted a place to call my own. I wanted a place that made me feel like all the hard work I was pouring in would be worth it. This location could help us grow our clientele because we'd look more official, so I emailed to set up a viewing.

JOURNAL ENTRY: 2013

As I walked into the old auto body shop on MLK and Hawthorne, I knew right away it was where I needed to be. They took the spray unit area and turned it into the coolest conference room I'd ever seen. The walls of the building are painted with murals, there's a lounge with couches, a kitchen, pool and ping pong table and a twenty-two-foot photo/video studio in the back. For $500 a month I can move in, have a table, and become a member.

I know I have to do it. This is how I grow—"Space creates opportunity"—I remember Hussein telling me. There's no way I can afford this place right now, but I'm willing to make any sacrifice to make it work. This is the first time in my life I'm going to do that. If it means not going out on weekends, staying late to make an extra sales call, whatever it is, I'm going to do it because I HAVE to. I'll be signing a six-month lease which means there are no off-months. I need this kick in the ass to take it to the next level.

Tonight is Sunday night; I have to have completed applications and a $500 deposit to him no later than Tuesday afternoon to secure the corner desk I want. I currently have $200 in the business account to put towards it with several jobs I should be picking up money for tomorrow.

> That money was supposed to go to the $800 debt I have on the business credit card from Fashion Fridays, the iPad, and San Diego flights, but I don't want to miss this opportunity. I'm paying him with the money I don't have and taking a full risk on myself.
>
> After the $500 is due, I'll owe him another $500 by the following Monday to start working and moving in. If I come back to this journal and talk about moving in and how awesome it is to be in this place, I guess we will know that somehow I figured it out. If not, then I wasn't able to swing it and mustn't have worked hard enough. Until then, I'll keep taking risks and learning from them. I've got to make moves, and this will be the biggest one of my life. Oh yeah, not to mention I owe my parents $125, Kayla $300, and still need to find health insurance on top of that.
>
> Grind mode starts today! There's no more time for excuses. I need to grow up, fend for myself, and go out there and make some money. I'm ready to grow, expand, and take hold of my life. I will forever live the exact experience I manifest because I believe in it and in myself. There's no way I can be stopped. Nothing. No way. No how. I'm proud of who I am, how I am, and can't wait until I grow into the man I know I'll be. I want to support my family, employ my sister so she can make what she's worth, give my parents something to do and keep them busy when they retire, and enjoy the time on Earth we have with each other. I'll never take them for granted and plan to do everything for other people in my life.

The space was 10,000 square feet with rows of desks and, after moving in, there was no one to be found. Turns out we were one of the first tenants and fell for the Craigslist ad fast, but either way the move still felt right. We agreed that no matter what projects we brought in, the first $500 would have to go toward rent. I signed the lease and took a huge bet on myself, knowing deep down in my core that this was the kick in the ass I needed. Not having a boss, I had to put pressure on myself to become uncomfortable and to grow. As for Kayla, she graciously let me stay a few more months before I packed up and moved back in with my parents, where I'd stay until figuring out my next steps.

The shared office was fantastic, and we loved the projects we started creating. It slowly became our community, and there were new and interesting people coming through the door every day. Every month, we'd hustle hard to find new screen-printing clients, finish up jobs, and collect payments so we could get rent paid on time.

Before I'd check my emails in the morning, I'd open QuickBooks, do my bookkeeping, and figure out exactly how much money we had and needed. Understanding our numbers would make or break our little business, so I made the conscious decision to stay on top of the finances and watch them like a hawk. There were many months when we barely had enough for rent, which left nothing to pay ourselves, but I never missed or was late on a payment. If my name was on a lease or contract, I was going to uphold my end of the deal.

The fact that I was working for myself and doing something interesting kept a smile on my face during my daily 35-minute drive. I woke up constantly excited for whatever challenges came my way and would seek out opportunities or moments to learn. One day we'd print shirts for a brand, and the next I'd learn about different inks, or a new style of shirt Wookie was working on, how much material went into pants, how to source it, or how to measure yardages. I learned about buckles, spent time on costing, and came to better understand invoicing timelines and how to manage client expectations and delivery dates. The list went on and on, and every day felt like school for me, except this time I was learning things that really mattered to my business. I wanted to become an expert on them.

I kept reading business books religiously—branding, marketing, taxes, biographies of business owners—and tried applying them to what I was experiencing every day in my new career. Sometimes, I'd mix up an order or print something wrong, costing us thousands of dollars, but every one of those mistakes became a moment to learn and get better for the next job. Nothing was ever a failure; it was all part of what I needed to learn to one day become successful.

We priced one job so poorly it ended up costing us nearly $7,000 to fix and replace. We completely botched the sample fees and labor costs and made the client's pants with the wrong pocket material. Our reputation was always more important than the money, so we did whatever we could to fix it, even though it took us almost six months to dig out of that hole.

* * *

After grinding for almost a year in the shared office, I started getting an itch to open our own space. The networking in our shared office turned out to be wonderful, but we'd worked hard to form an identity of our own around town, and when clients walked in, they were often confused by what a "shared office space" was.

I looked on Craigslist again and found a 650-square-foot studio office in Oldtown that looked perfect! Compound, the largest streetwear shop in Portland, was across the street, and I wanted to be near their energy and customer base. When Wookie and I arrived for the tour at 412 NW Couch Street Suite 20, we opened the door and knew it was home. Looking at white walls with a small kitchen in the corner, I could already envision the future HQ of Creative 35 in my head.

The problem was that rent would be $1,500 per month, and I wasn't sure we could afford it. I knew Creative 35 needed this location to expand and was willing to do whatever it took to make the extra money to see it through, but we'd need to hustle even harder if we wanted to make this place a reality. I knew the opportunities a space of our own could generate and figured if I could get a few people to help share the rent, we'd be able to make it work.

I had a vision for what I wanted the space to look like, so I strategically invited a few people I thought would add value to it. I called our friend D. J. Willingham, a sneaker collector and early member of Creative 35 who owned a consignment site called Flight Skool. Having lots of sneaker boxes around would add to the vibe I was trying to achieve, and D. J. was a well-networked guy Wookie and I liked hanging around with. The other guy was Everett (@illgander on Instagram), an up-and-coming photographer with an amazing eye who'd be able to snap photos of our projects as needed. Both guys jumped at the opportunity, and we all agreed to split the rent three ways.

Over the coming months, Wookie and I began getting into a groove and learned how we could grow our business and make sure the lights stayed on. Always on the lookout for new jobs, I'd attend every event I could to meet new people and grow my community connections and reputation. At one event, I met a nice lady who worked as an assistant for Dorell Wright, a Trail

Blazer. She invited us to Wright's poutine-eating contest fundraiser for his foundation. The young Blazer-loving kid inside me lit up at the opportunity to possibly meet a player, and after Wookie and I made the five-block walk from our office to Deschutes Brewery in the Pearl, we were surprised to see only fifteen people in attendance.

I'd expected hundreds to be there, and instead, suddenly I was sitting just ten feet away from Blazer players Dorell Wright, Wesley Matthews, Thomas Robinson, and our newest rookie draft pick, C. J. McCollum.

After thirty minutes of sitting and watching the players eat, text on their phones, and watch SportsCenter on the TVs, I mustered up the courage to walk over and introduce myself. I had nothing to lose and everything to gain—so I figured, why not?

Dressed in custom Jaefields clothes, I introduced myself to Wesley Matthews and C. J. McCollum and told them we did full custom apparel and would love to have them visit our office a few blocks down. "Think of it as the Nike ID of clothes," I said. "We'd love to have you swing by our showroom sometime to check out what we do!"

They didn't seem very into it, but I left them with business cards anyway, exchanged phone numbers with C. J., and went on my way.

Sitting in our office weeks later, I received a call from a phone number with a Wisconsin area code, and I picked up.

"Marcus?" a deep voice said on the other end.

"Yes? Who's this?"

"It's Wesley Matthews of the Blazers. We're downstairs."

I looked at Wookie with shock on my face.

"They're here..." I said.

I peeked out the window, and parked right below us was a brand new, blacked-out Range Rover. As we scrambled to clean the office, I heard a knock on the door and opened it, and standing there were Wesley and his buddy, who'd come to see what Creative 35 was all about.

Never would I have thought a business card would bring an NBA player to our office.

I went into full sales mode as I began showing Wesley projects we'd done, different types of material we used, and how we could help make him clothes that would stand out. At times during my rant, Wesley looked at his buddy like, "What are we doing here?" But as I kept selling, I could tell we were making progress.

After a while, Wesley shared that he wanted to screen-print a few shirts under a brand name he'd been thinking of called "Undrafted." He came out of college and had to work his ass off to make an NBA team and this experience was something he, and lots of other athletes, carried with them.

We took Wesley's measurements, we talked more about his style and what he'd like to see, and then he went on his way. I told him we'd text him when we had things to show him, and after a few weeks of back and forth, I went to his house to drop off custom shirts and pants for his upcoming road trip. Pulling up to an NBA player's house in my old Mitsubishi Lancer ignited a spark in me to keep working hard so I could one day afford a car I wouldn't be embarrassed to drive. I wanted to belong in Wesley Matthews' crowd, and this day at his home would be my first step.

I dropped off a handful of custom Wookie-designed clothes and swiped his card for $2,000. In that one transaction, we'd just made enough to pay two months of rent.

Over the coming year, we ended up doing a good amount of work for Wesley and would often see him walking into games rocking our gear or hanging with his friends wearing an "Undrafted" tee we had made. I also started to work on building a relationship with C. J. McCollum, the Blazers' new rookie, whom I thought might be a good person to know in the future.

LIFE LESSONS LEARNED

- → Space creates opportunity.
- → Search for moments when your back feels against the wall.
- → Share your desires with the world.
- → Know your numbers.
- → Get good at selling.

CHAPTER 9

@PORTLAND

IN 2014, I WAS GROWING AS AN ENTREPRENEUR AND loving what I was doing, but I still didn't have a solid plan for what my next move would be or how to fully monetize my skills. My mom knew I was on a good path but worried about how I would continue to take care of myself without a secure job and paycheck.

I asked her, "What would I have to do to make you feel like I'm successful and you don't have to worry about me?"

She replied, "As long as you can pay your bills and have health insurance, I won't worry."

That was the final push I needed to move out and fully figure things out on my own. I needed the pressure to succeed, and renting an apartment seemed like the inevitable next step. I reached out to friends and clients, expressed my desire to move downtown, and asked them to let me know about any opportunities. Turns out the client whose job I'd made the $7,000 mistake on had an extra room in his low-income housing building that I could move into right away.

I said yes.

It was an interesting adjustment from living in a comfortable family home to living with people of all ages, backgrounds, disabilities, and income levels. If I wanted to have guests over, they'd have to check in at the front and submit a copy of their ID in case any crimes were committed.

There always seemed to be a story to tell in that building, including the one about the time I found a man by himself in the elevator having a heart attack and had to call 9-1-1 and help him to safety.

Living there never felt like home, but it was a needed stepping-stone toward where I wanted to be. Being close to work, I woke up at 6:30 a.m. and was in the office by 7 every morning, trying to get a jump on the day and find us a new paying client. I began loving the hustle, and the hour I saved commuting every day allowed me to get an extra hour of work done, which helped nurture the business.

As our client list grew and people started to notice us around town, I saw how popular Instagram had become and understood it as a possible impactful tool for us to utilize. I'd been using the app since it first launched while I was in college, and I enjoyed taking pictures and sharing them with others. I started an account for Creative 35 where every day I'd try to post a picture of something we were working on in hopes that it would build demand for our services, foster a sense of community, or

@PORTLAND

tell a story that people wanted to be part of. I could tell from the beginning this application could have power.

Sitting one night watching TV, I scrolled through Instagram mindlessly and came across an account named @seattle. I clicked on it and saw beautiful photos of the city, skyline, Space Needle, local food, and cool things to do in town. I thought this page was insightful, interesting, and engaging, so I looked for the Portland equivalent.

There was nothing to be found.

The @portland handle was taken by a guy on the East Coast who posted pictures of his daughters, but there weren't any pages showcasing Portland and all its beauty.

I had an eye for photography and enjoyed using Instagram. If I couldn't find an account featuring my beloved city, I'd start one myself! I came up with the username @portlandnw for northwest, which was short, memorable, and had a matching hashtag—#portlandnw—that had been used zero times.

That night I posted my first photo of a bike along the waterfront, used a bunch of hashtags to get people's attention, and said, "What a beautiful shot of the Broadway Bridge. Be sure to tag #portlandnw to be featured!"

Instagram was an interactive app, and I'd seen how some pages utilized featured content to grow. I figured it would be a great way not only to increase my following, but also to get excellent content for free. I could vary posts between pictures of bridges, coffee, beer, the river, and cool, local up-and-coming brands. If I could create a page that amazing photographers would want to see their images featured on, I could potentially gain an audience and a notable page without having to take and edit the photos myself.

> ### JOURNAL ENTRY: 2014
>
> I've been working on this new @portlandnw Instagram page for ten weeks now, and it's already at 8,000 followers! I started it as a way to promote all the Portland brands we're working with, and to share photos of this incredible city with tips on things to do and where to hang out, but I can already tell it's growing into something bigger.
>
> This morning there was a shooting at Reynolds High School in Portland, so I decided to design an image and post it to show my condolences and sadness. I posted it this morning under #prayforreynolds, and by 5 p.m., it has nearly 800 reposts. My mom said KGW news did a segment on it and shared my image on TV. I think the power of social media is at an all-time high.

As I continued building the @portlandnw page over the following months, it quickly grew from zero to twenty-five thousand followers. If I could just get that @portland handle from the guy on the East Coast, it would be like having Portland.com, and I could see the page growing even faster!

I sent him a direct message and asked if he'd be interested in selling the handle. Within an hour, he replied "no."

I stayed on him, not willing to take no for an answer, and after a few weeks of back and forth, finally convinced him to name his price. He replied, "$5,000."

I was hustling as hard as I could for brands, people, and organizations, but that number was just too far out of reach. I couldn't afford that price for a username when I was hardly making any money and had both rents due in the next five days.

I countered at $500 and explained that all I wanted to do was post cool pictures of my city; after a week of silence, he got back to me and said, "$1,500."

I could tell he was reluctant to move on from it. I couldn't help but notice how much he posted about his daughters. I replied one last time and said, "Look, the most I can do is $1,000. That's a lot of money for me, and all you have to do is add an underscore to your username. With that money you can take your daughters to Disneyland on a nice trip!"

I couldn't believe it, but my Disney move worked—he said yes! The only stipulation was that he needed half the money up front before he would trade the name. However, the real problem was that I barely had $1,000 to *my* name. I would be sending him all of my money—savings, business account dollars, the piggy bank, everything. I couldn't miss this opportunity.

I hustled hard to close the deal as fast as possible and told him I'd like to meet him over Skype before sending him the $500 deposit. There's no official way to change an Instagram name, so I recommended we change our usernames live, over Skype, at the exact same time. The second after he added the underscore (_) to his username and changed it to @portland_, I would delete the NW from @portlandnw and press enter to officially claim the @portland handle.

Sitting at my family dinner table, I Skyped with him at 6 a.m. in hopes that as few people as possible would be on Instagram and I'd have a chance to take that username during the one second it would be available between accounts. I sent him the deposit, he confirmed, and it was time for the switch. I watched him type it in, I typed in mine, and we counted down from three.

Three...

Two...

I had no idea if this crazy process I'd come up with would work, but the reward was worth the risk.

One...

He hit "Send" first. Then I did, and...

It worked.

There it was, my new username, @portland; and his, @portland_. We were both able to keep our followers, resulting in a seamless and perfect transition. I couldn't believe it. I thanked him for his time, told him to enjoy Disneyland, and ended the Skype call.

Within minutes of having the new username, the page seemed to come alive! People naturally began posting photos and tagging @portland without even realizing it was my page.

In under three months, the page grew to sixty thousand followers—all Portland-loving people just like me, from all over the world. I realized quickly that I was onto something big, and this page could be used to help build my reputation and my career. Sixty thousand people following something I created was a lot, and I had to really sit and understand that these were real people just like you and me who were searching for community and a sense of belonging.

I tested the reach by hosting an event called "PDX MEET" in a great Pearl District space I found and invited local artists, musicians, bands, and photographers to join. I planned photo walks around town with local creatives, hosted events, and tried my best to utilize this digital platform to create meaningful real-life connection.

I feel joy and comfort when I'm surrounded by people who love the same things I love. From childhood wearing the Oregon O and Nike swoosh, to high school and the Keller Krew tee, to my college years with Updrift, seeing people around me enjoying themselves and coming together because of a unifying cause has become my mission. I want others to feel safe and welcomed when they're surrounded by me and my people, and this Instagram page was proving to be a great way to share moments with others.

LIFE LESSONS LEARNED

- → It takes sacrifice to realize your dreams.
- → High risk equals high reward.
- → Trust your vision.
- → Everything's negotiable.
- → Community is key.

CHAPTER 10

HACKED

AFTER A FEW MONTHS OF LIVING IN LOW-INCOME HOUS-ing, it was time to look for a new spot. After a quick Craigslist search, I chose the cheapest place I could find on the West Side and signed a lease with my college best friend, Eli, who had recently moved back to town after graduating.

The Yards at Union Station was inexpensive and located right next to the train tracks where trains would pass by blaring at all hours of the night. Our windows faced the tracks, and the rumble and grinding of the engines would make you jump out of your seat.

Living along the waterfront, I ran the loop as often as I could to take in Portland and enjoy the warming weather. On one run, I decided to leave my phone on my bed so I could disconnect for a while and let my mind wander. When I got home and opened Instagram, my @portland username had been changed to @portland9999999.

My heart sank when I realized I'd been hacked.

Suddenly, a new @portland Instagram page with zero followers and my username was in use and starting to post pictures just like I'd done. This page had become such a part of my identity that I freaked out. I didn't know what to do next. Not only did I have money invested, but I'd also spent hundreds and hundreds of hours building this page and creating community by bringing people together.

I changed my username back to @portlandnw, hoping people would recognize it when I posted for help, and quickly designed a post:

"We've been hacked, and I need your help! Someone took my username and started a new @portland page, and I need you all to go to that page and start commenting on Instagram that this was stolen!"

The new @portland page started posting the exact same photos I'd posted and even used my hashtags. A few minutes later, up popped a direct message from the new @portland page that read:

"Every empire must fall. You've had your run."

I didn't understand what this meant or who was trying to take me down.

After I posted the photo asking for help, the community I'd worked so hard to create came to my rescue. I'd spent so much of my time making this page, building the community, creating content, and hosting events for others, and it felt amazing that strangers wanted to help me get it back. Over the next few weeks, I was able to get in contact with someone at Instagram through a friend, and after sending over lots of emails, verifications, and even head shot photos of Eli and me to prove our faces had been seen on the page, I was given the handle back.

That moment changed me.

To see something I'd worked so hard to create be taken away in an instant made me start thinking and looking at business differently. Even though we sign up for these apps and use our own photos and names, we don't own them. They live in some weird space, and months and years of hard work can be taken away or deleted in a snap. I realized, right then and there, that I needed to make something real and tangible that no one could take away. I would use Instagram and @portland as a tool to help build something bigger. Much bigger.

* * *

Living downtown, I became familiar with the local streetwear shops and boutiques. One day, while visiting a friend working at a denim shop, I came across an old-school, vintage baseball hat with a simple letter P on it. I purchased the hat and started rocking it as my "Portland hat" since I couldn't find anything to wear at the time that expressed my Portland pride. I loved the simplicity of it and that it went with anything I wore. I began wearing the hat daily, and it became part of my look and identity for over three months.

Portland didn't have a Major League Baseball team, something that often provided an unofficial city logo. Think the Yankees' NY logo for New York, or the Dodgers' LA-stacked icon for Los

Angeles. Being a local kid and sports junkie, I missed having a simple logo to show off my hometown pride. I loved the Trail Blazers, Timbers, and Thorns, but those were more graphics and icons to me than a logo that represented the identity of Portland. I wanted to wear something clean and straightforward, something that would look cool next to my two favorite logos, the Nike Swoosh and the Oregon O.

Wookie and I had been in our office, working on other clients' projects, slowly growing his Jaefields company, but my itch to have a brand and store of my own had intensified. I'd fallen in love with retail and servicing customers when I'd worked at the Nike Employee Store; I loved the intersection between people and products, and how people relate to and experience the things they buy. For years, I'd watched brands like Johnny Cupcakes, Supreme, and Kith and dreamed of having a store and a line of people around the block waiting to get in on opening day. I wanted to experience this for myself and would manifest it in my thoughts and dreams daily.

I was realizing that all the things I loved in life and was searching for were quickly coming together.

→ Sixty thousand followers on Instagram who loved Portland
→ wearing my "P" hat every day to show my Portland pride
→ Portland not having a baseball team or logo for the city
→ my Instagram page being hacked and wanting to create something tangible
→ an ability to design simple websites and knowledge of photography
→ clients requesting that their contract-printed shirts have "Made in Portland" on the labels

- → a love for brands and storytelling
- → a degree in graphic design
- → years of experience in the screen-printing industry
- → a deep desire to create something for myself

I had come a long way from making my first shirt in high school. I knew in that moment I was ready, and it was once again time to bet on myself.

I opened Adobe Illustrator like I did ten times a day, but this time it felt different. I had a mission and conviction that I was about to make something important and meaningful. I decided it was time to make a brand for the city, apparel I would want to wear to show my Rose City pride.

Since designing my first shirt in high school, my style had always been simple because, frankly, I didn't have the skillset to make complex designs. I found myself drawn to brands and logos that were clean, easy to wear, and made a bold statement.

Simple was pleasing to me, and simple made sense.

I loved the P hat I'd been wearing the past few months and how a simple logo could represent Portland. I started looking through fonts I had on my computer to find something that stood out but looked intentional. It would also need to be just a one-color design since that was most cost-effective for screen printing and embroidery.

I started with a blocky P letter from an athletic high school font I found and played with the line width, angles, and shape. I wanted it thicker than the font on my screen, so I brought up the line stoke and began to pull rulers from the side of my artboard to proportionately reshape the letter with new boldness. I quickly noticed that by adding thickness and blocks to the bottom, it started to look like a real logo.

Although I wanted simple, it was too simple at this point and needed something more. I started thinking of other elements to add or ways to change the P. With Wookie over my shoulder providing his ever-positive feedback, we noted that the inside of the P looked like a square, and that the state of Oregon might fit into the dead space. I pulled an Oregon outline from Google, traced it, and placed it into the letter.

In that moment, the P logo was born.

I liked what I saw on my screen, but I wasn't fully convinced it would become anything big—or even that it was exactly what I was hoping to design. It looked unique and interesting, but I wanted to get feedback from a few people I trusted before doing anything more.

I'd recently met a designer named Brian whose style I'd come to respect and appreciate, and I sent him my concept before leaving for a family trip to Hawaii.

EMAIL: OCTOBER 30, 2014

Brian, I'm not sure if I love what I came up with here, but I think it's at least a good start. Can you keep playing with it and see if you can come up with anything better? Please see logo attached.

Lying next to the pool with my family in Hawaii, I saw a call from Brian pop up on my phone.

"Hello?"

"I think you already have it, man. I wouldn't change a thing," Brian said.

"Are you sure?"

"Yeah, I've played with it some but can't come up with anything better. This is a cool design."

I sent the logo for feedback to my representative at Oregon Screen Impressions, a local screen print shop I'd recently begun working with. She replied, "I've worked here twenty years and have printed nearly every design for this city. I can't believe I've never seen this concept for a logo before. I think you're onto something."

With both of their approvals and Black Friday only a few weeks away, I decided it was time to pull the trigger and begin making a few products to try selling. Black Friday was the biggest spending day of the year and a perfect day to launch my new designs. I had nothing to lose and, worst-case scenario, I'd give them away to my family and friends as gifts if no one bought them.

A year earlier, I'd become very interested in purchasing domain names, hoping I'd make money by flipping them for a profit. I couldn't afford a house, so instead, I'd buy what I called "digital real estate." For $9 a year, I'd secure good domain names and sit on them in hopes someone would email me asking to purchase. It was my get-rich-quick plan. I'd spend hours and hours researching cool names or heavily searched terms, trying to find a jackpot to secure and sit on for a later date.

One day, I went deep into Portland(fill in the blank).com domains. I bought everything from PortlandTequilla.com to PortlandSocks.com. By the end of the day, I'd purchased nearly thirty domains in the hopes a few would eventually catch on.

Twenty-nine never did, but one made it all worthwhile.

When it was time to name this new "P" project, I started thinking about all the different words and phrases I could use to describe it. I knew from experience that this brand needed to have the name Portland in it, as I'd be growing it from the @portland Instagram page. I wanted the brand to be about wearing Portland. It needed to be able to encapsulate the various items I might one day want to offer. I thought about Portlandshirts.com but realized that would make it hard to sell hats and accessories, and Portlandapparel.com just didn't have a good ring to it.

Using Thesaurus.com, I researched words that described multiple items. "Gear" was one of the terms I found, and I liked it. I thought Portland Gear sounded good and could also encompass a lot of different product categories I might find my way into one day. I typed portlandgear.com into GoDaddy and discovered it was taken. I tried looking up who owned it but couldn't find any information.

I continued my search for available words and domains, but Portland Gear was stuck in my head.

After a few more hours of searching and trying other word combinations, I opened my spreadsheet of domains I already owned and noticed that *I* was the one who had portlandgear.com. I laughed out loud and realized this was the sign I needed.

I'd call my company Portland Gear.

JOURNAL ENTRY: 2014

With the success of the Portland page, and me knowing product and branding, I'm taking on my first solo project, "Portland Gear." I want to make amazing simple and branded Portland clothing that's sold around town to create community. I know people want a piece of Portland, so I'm going to give it to them! When you travel you see so many people wanting a shirt, pen, mug, and there just isn't anyone in Portland doing it right, until now! I've come up with some really cool logos I'll look to get trademarked and will build it all through the @portland page I have. I want it to be the next great Portland company and place all the locals go. I know Portland has it in it to embrace a brand like this. People are really starting to flock to this town, I want to help make it cool!

LIFE LESSONS LEARNED

- → Build things to last.
- → People will challenge you. Know your truths.
- → Trust the opinions of people you respect.
- → Do more of what you love.
- → When you have nothing to lose, it means you have everything to gain.

CHAPTER 11

VALIDATION

IT WAS ALMOST TIME TO LAUNCH PORTLAND GEAR, SO I did what I thought every entrepreneur did: find an investor. For years, I had watched Shark Tank, and I truthfully thought it was the only way to start if I was going to make my company successful.

While working in the shared office on MLK years prior, I'd met a gentleman who liked investing in local projects. Other than what I'd learned from Shark Tank, I didn't know how to value my idea or what it really meant to get an investment. I had no clue about how much money I'd need, what I'd spend it on, or if I even would *need* to spend it. I just thought it was what you did.

Remembering when I'd told my first web client that I charged $90 an hour, I aimed high and threw out a huge number—because, why not?

I asked for $70,000 in exchange for 30 percent of this "idea" that I was yet to actually bring to life. He'd seen me work in the office and knew my work ethic, but this number wasn't based on anything; it was just a gut feeling, and I'd need him to feel the same way.

For years I'd been nose-down, grinding, hardly ever making a profit—so $70,000 sounded like $70 million to me. If I could secure a deal with him, I truthfully felt I'd be set for life. I didn't care about how much equity I was giving up since it was technically worth nothing; I just wanted to get a deal done, see that money in the bank, and say, "I have an investor" to my friends and family.

After sending off the email, I didn't hear back for a few weeks. Then, randomly, my potential investor and his business partner asked to meet up. He was interested in more than just Portland Gear; he wanted to invest in me as a person, and he knew from watching me around the office over the last year that I'd make this idea happen. He liked all the projects I was working on and wanted to keep them together.

Not only did he offer me money, but he offered more than what I had asked for: $100,000 in exchange for 30 percent of Portland Gear and the @portland Instagram page.

Sitting with them at Theo's burger place in Old Town, I was overcome with joy and felt I'd just won the lottery. Trying to keep my cool and look professional, I thanked them and asked for some time to think about it. All those years of grinding, taking risks, and putting myself in positions to succeed were about to pay off.

* * *

I thought long and hard about the offer, but something just wasn't sitting right. I realized that in starting Portland Gear, my motivator had never been money. It was to create something that I was proud to wear and that helped bring people together, not to get rich or have partners.

I wanted to solve a personal problem I was having—not being able to wear and share my Portland pride—and I wanted other people to be proud of their hometown just like I was. After thinking more, I realized it wasn't going to require very much money to start. I understood the margin and printing times in apparel and knew that with hard work and hustle I'd be able to grow it organically and not need a rocket of money behind it.

I countered, and we agreed over a handshake on $60,000 in exchange for 10 percent of just Portland Gear, not the @portland page.

Although it was less than the $100,000 I could have received, $60,000 was still more money than I'd ever seen in my life, and it felt like I'd just won the business lottery. Also, having to give up 10 percent felt much better than 30 percent.

When I walked into the bank with my $60,000 check to Portland Gear, I experienced another moment of unforgettable validation. To have someone believe in not only the product I was going to create, but also in me as a human, was both humbling and scary. Depositing that check on November 20, 2014, put me on a mission to launch Portland Gear and make my family, friends, investor, and community proud.

Sixty thousand dollars would be plenty to get the project off the ground, purchase inventory, invest in marketing, and keep a bunch extra in the reserves for a rainy day. My mindset from the beginning was to spend as little as possible, because I felt it wasn't my money to lose in the first place. I wanted to be a responsible business owner and steward of the funds I'd been given.

With cash in the bank, the P and P(or)tland logos done, and less than ten days until Black Friday, it was full steam ahead.

After working on various client brands over the years, I knew what I wanted my brand to be like—but, more importantly, not to be like. I wasn't going to order a bunch of the same shirt in different colors or come out with too many designs. Both avenues would turn into inventory nightmares and inevitable discounting. Instead, I had two T-shirt designs I liked that were basic, simple, and easy for everyone to wear. It would be my job to convince people these were the designs to have. This brand was my art, and I wanted people to see and experience it as I intended.

A heather-navy tee with an off-white P on the front left chest, and PORTLAND 1845 OREGON on the back, would be my main shirt; and a black tee with a white Portland and an Oregon-shaped outline around the "OR" would be my second. I ordered fifty-eight of each shirt (which got me a price break for hitting a higher volume) and figured if I didn't sell them, I could always give them to fraternity brothers, friends, or family. I also felt good about these numbers because I'd hardly be spending any of my investor's money, so in a worst-case scenario, I could return all of it and personally pay back what I had lost.

VALIDATION

I asked Everett, the most talented photographer I knew—and a Creative 35 member—if he'd help me shoot a few photos of the two items so I could launch them the following week. He reached out to a model friend, Jaida, and I talked to Eli, asking if they'd be willing to model for free. They said yes.

We loaded up the car and headed out around town for what would become the first-ever Portland Gear photo shoot. With two T-shirt designs, we walked around the leaf-covered, rainy city for a few hours, taking photos in various locations to show the variety of places in which people could rock our gear. We shot at Voodoo Doughnuts, Cathedral Park, Old Town, and the waterfront, all of which were iconic Portland areas that I felt would resonate with our potential customers. When people thought of Portland Gear, I wanted them to associate it with the beauty of our city.

Everett edited the pictures, and I uploaded them to a Shopify website I'd just finished building the night before. For $29 a month, this platform would keep track of all my e-commerce orders, inventory, customers, and everything I needed to get the brand off the ground.

I texted my Dad in Hillsboro, asking if he could test portlandgear.com and place an order to make sure it worked. It did, and so he became our very first customer.

It was time to introduce the world to my brand.

LIFE LESSONS LEARNED

- → Know your numbers.
- → Think long-term and take time to research business structures.
- → When others believe in you, it builds confidence.
- → Utilize your network.
- → Start simple.

CHAPTER 12

LAUNCH AND LOVE

DRIVING TO MY OFFICE, IT FELT LIKE CHRISTMAS MORN-ing. I was filled with anticipation, but I was also nervous about how the day would go. I had portlandgear.com ready, 116 T-shirts to sell, and a Dropbox folder of images to share with the world. My @portland page had grown to sixty thousand followers, and I felt hopeful that people would respond to the brand in a positive way.

At 9 a.m., I posted the first-ever image of a Portland Gear item to the world.

"Due to the overwhelming interest in Portland, we decided Black Friday was the perfect time to release the official apparel line of @portland. To help share your love for Portland, we're launching two unisex Portland tees. Use code BLACK FRIDAY to receive 20 percent off until 3 PM PST. Link in the bio. Follow @portlandgear for new products and updates. #portlandnw #portlandgear."

As I sat alone in my cold Old Town office, patiently watching the computer screen for an order to come in, nothing happened. After ten minutes of zero orders, I felt a bit discouraged and heard the Thanksgiving parade going by outside, so I decided to close my computer and go for a walk.

With cold rain rolling down my face, feeling bummed and defeated that no one shared my vision for a wearable Portland brand, I began taking photos of the parade to post on the @portland page. I had made it to Pioneer Square to post up and watch the parade go by when I heard a sound on my phone.

Cha-ching.

What was that? I thought.

I looked at my phone's screen and saw my first order had come in.

Success!!

Someone bought something. I wonder who it was!

As I opened my phone to see the order—*cha-ching, cha-ching, cha-ching. Cha-ching.*

Suddenly, the chiming wouldn't stop.

I took off running against the flow of the parade, dodging spectators, with the biggest smile on my face as I realized people found value in what I'd created. I sprinted into the office and turned on my computer. I couldn't believe what was happening.

Fifteen orders in the last five minutes, and now they were starting to pour in! Portland, Washington, New York, California—I was seeing addresses and names I'd never seen before!

I knew this day was about to turn into one I'd never want to forget, so I started taking a running tally of sales.

**BLACK FRIDAY TIMELINE:
NOVEMBER 28, 2014**

9:00 AM—launched Portland Gear on @portlandgear: 1 photo

9:30 AM—$287, 8 orders, @portlandgear: 0 followers

10:00 AM—$825.20, 18 orders, @portlandgear: 220 followers

10:15 AM—$921.20, 20 orders, @portlandgear: 240 followers

10:35 AM—$1,032, 22 orders, @portlandgear: 280 followers

11:00 AM—$1,262, 30 orders, @portlandgear: 315 followers

11:30 AM—$1,515, 38 orders, @portlandgear: 336 followers

12:30 PM—$1,837, 46 orders, @portlandgear: 392 followers

1:00 PM—$1,984, 50 orders, @portlandgear: 400 followers

4:15 PM—$3,891, 105 orders, @portlandgear: 575 followers

8:30 PM—$4,400, 118 orders, @portlandgear: 646 followers

11:30 PM—$4,949, 121 orders, @portlandgear: 700 followers

By late afternoon, I'd done nearly $2,000 in sales and figured I'd post again for all the people who had missed the first one.

"Only two hours left in our inaugural Black Friday special and @portlandgear launch. Head to portlandgear.com to purchase one of the very first Portland tees. Use code BLACK FRIDAY for 20 percent off. #portlandnw #portlandgear."

Cha-ching, cha-ching, cha-ching.

The orders started to roll in again. I was in absolute shock. Four hours ago, nobody in the world had heard of Portland Gear or been to my website, and now, with two posts, I was shipping fifty orders out to people and places I'd never heard of.

As excited as I was to be selling this much product, I now had two problems: (1) I had never shipped an order from Shopify before, and (2) I didn't have enough inventory to send. I'd oversold every size.

I called my screen printer to see if they could quickly produce more and if they'd be willing to help me ship, and they said yes to both.

From nothing but a box of tees and a folder of images to over 120 orders, new followers, email addresses, customer service emails, and $5,000 in sales, I felt like I was onto something.

Something big.

By the end of the first day, I knew this was going to be my thing. I was willing and able to do whatever it took to keep this momentum going and create product for the people of Portland. I was 100 percent committed to making this my full-time, every-second-of-the-day job, and I wanted to see it grow.

In creating this brand, all I'd wanted was to be able to wear my Portland pride; and after only one day, I realized other people wanted to do the same thing.

* * *

Although I had a few girlfriends in high school and college, none of the relationships ever got very serious, and now I was feeling lonely and wanting to give love. I had a big heart, and with so much happening in my life so quickly, wanted a partner to experience it with.

While living at my sister's, my parents', in low-income housing, and at The Yards, at night I'd often pray for God to give me someone to share this journey with. I had a weird feeling in my core that I was destined for something unique with my life, and I wanted a partner who'd be with me from the beginning—someone to share the ups and the downs that were inevitably going to come my way.

I'd often catch my mind wandering. *Isn't it crazy that the person I'm going to marry is alive right now? They're doing something, they're living, working, and we just don't know each other yet! I can't wait to meet her.*

A year earlier, I'd been having lunch with my friend Savannah at McMenamins on NW 21st Street when a cute blonde girl named Noelle drove by, jumped out to say hi to Savannah, and walked away. In our two-minute exchange I knew there was something different about her, and I half-jokingly told Savannah I was going to marry that girl one day.

She just seemed perfect.

Exactly one week after I launched Portland Gear, on December 5, 2014, Savannah invited me out to celebrate that very girl's birthday. I didn't feel like going out that night, as I was tired from working all day; but since they were only two blocks away from where I was living, I doused myself in cologne, tossed on my Portland hat, and walked to meet up.

Upon walking in, I saw her in a beautiful sequined dress, and my heart started to race. I tried the "cool guy" approach all night by talking to everyone else in the group except her, but all I wanted was to find a reason to pull her aside. As the night went on, I continued buying drinks for everyone, hoping it would catch her attention and I'd appear to be the life of the party, but it didn't work.

Right at the end of the night, she joined Savannah and me on the couch to say hello. Heart fluttering, I struck up a conversation with her, and I suddenly didn't want the night to end.

Sitting there that night, I knew one day I truly was going to marry her. I had no doubt in my mind she was the perfect person for me, and I was about to do whatever it took to convince her I was meant for her.

After a few days of texting, I finally mustered up the courage and asked her to go out on a Christmas-themed date. I took her to dinner, ice skating at Lloyd Center, Salt & Straw, and the famous Pioneer Square Christmas tree. We walked around talking for hours—neither of us wanting to leave.

I had just designed the P hoodie and asked her if she'd be

interested in taking pictures the next day for this new brand I'd started called Portland Gear. She said yes, and I told her to meet me at Mother's Bistro for breakfast the next day.

I was already head-over-heels in love.

Noelle and I have been together ever since that day in 2014, and I'm so lucky and proud to call her my wife. God answered my prayers, and Noelle has been with me every single step of the way, always loving me for who I am and supporting me in what I do. She even lived with Eli and me when our living room was floor-to-ceiling hat boxes, and she never complained or said a word. You could always find her by my side at pop-up events, Blazer games, or photo shoots, and her presence made me feel like I could chase my dreams with no restraints. She gave me superpowers.

* * *

Noelle and I got married on August 18, 2018, under an old oak tree in front of two hundred of our closest friends, family members, and employees. I love Noelle more than anything in the world and am sure thankful God answered my prayers. In August of 2021, we welcomed our daughter Kinley to the family and have cherished every second together.

LIFE LESSONS LEARNED

- → Share your creation with the world. It will open doors you never knew existed.
- → When you know, you know. Trust your gut.
- → Appreciate those who support and love you for who you are.

- → Find a healthy balance of personal life and work.
- → Jump headfirst into love and never hold back.

CHAPTER 13

BUILDING COMMUNITY

THE MINUTE I LAUNCHED PORTLAND GEAR, I KNEW IT'D be my full-time job. I devoted every second to it. Seeing sales increase leading up to the holiday was exciting! Orders continued coming in every day, and I started dreaming and thinking about what I'd need to do next to keep the momentum going.

The Portland Saturday Market was a big deal in town, and I knew we'd have a good chance at selling our product there if I could just get in front of the right people. I registered for a booth in the back for $150 and purchased a tent, table, and rack to do my first-ever event. I needed help, and since Eli was off on the weekends, I asked him to tag along; he said yes.

Although Eli was a few years younger than me, we grew close during my last two years at the University of Oregon. After graduation, he'd moved home to Portland and was hired at an executive event-planning company. The years we lived together in our apartment at The Yards were some of the fondest of my life. We were young and broke but having fun living in a big city and experiencing adulting for the first time. We'd walk the bridge to Moda Center for Blazers games and concerts and were known for bumping the latest Justin Bieber in Apartment 407.

As people walked by our pop-up, we'd draw them in by offering free stickers or temporary tattoos in hopes they'd listen to us tell the Portland Gear story and maybe buy a shirt to support us.

Almost every person who heard the story would end up buying something. The more we shared, the more we sold.

* * *

My second date with Noelle was at a coffee shop. She brought her Bible, and I brought a blank piece of paper to think of new Portland Gear ideas.

I knew Portland Gear was always going to be a community-based brand, so I began thinking of creative ways to get my product in front of the people of Portland and not just online through social media. Going back to the Nike story, I remembered reading that Geoff Hollister, a former Nike employee, and Phil Knight drove around in the early 1970s in a VW bus and sold sneakers out of the back at local track meets. They knew their customers could be found at these events, so they took the product directly to them, making the sale easier.

My dream was to one day open a retail store, but after only a few weeks in, I knew it wasn't viable yet. I'd barely sold $10,000 in product, and very few people had even heard of my brand. There was a lot of work to be done.

If I could create something mobile like Nike, and take my product to potential Portland customers, it just might work. Instead of trying to reinvent or develop a cool new concept, I thought it would align perfectly with my Nike upbringing to purchase the same vehicle and hit the same roads as a tribute.

I pulled out my phone, began looking on Craigslist for old Volkswagen buses, and came across a beautiful 1973 Westfalia pop-top painted mustard yellow.

The next day, in an East Portland backyard, I peeled back a mossy tarp and saw this beautiful vehicle for the first time. Complete with daisy plaid curtains, mustard-yellow seat fabric to match the exterior, old wood panels, and cabinets that folded down, I knew I had to have it.

With some of the initial investor's money, I purchased the bus for $10,000 and drove it home to The Yards. I had plans to rebuild the interior to make it custom, something that would be more eye-catching and work better for these mobile pop-up shops I wanted to do. The goal of this bus was to be seen, make noise, and draw people in to take pictures with it. If I could create something people would want to post a photo of on their social media, it would help spread the word about Portland Gear for free. I decided it needed a bright teal wrap with big text letters, and fun Portland designs.

As the bus remodel neared completion, I began reaching out to upcoming events to host my first mobile pop-up. I cold-emailed TEDxPortland and inquired about getting involved. TEDxPortland is one of the most inspirational and educational days for the city all year, and I knew their community would find interest in my brand.

The curator, David Rae, said they'd love to have the Portland Gear bus parked outside as a symbol of the event being about Portland, and that I could sell whatever products I had.

It would become my first event with our bus.

As I pulled up that morning, people could not stop staring. All day long, potential customers approached and asked about the bus, what year it was, what my brand was all about, and if I was selling anything that they could buy and support. I stood there and told my story to every person who'd listen, knowing these interactions would become memorable connections and help create an emotional tie to the brand.

I could tell right away that pop-ups and getting the brand out in the city would help authenticate us as "Portland" and grow our roots within the city. I knew there'd be long days ahead standing behind the bus, slinging shirts—but it was working, and I was willing to do it.

I saw online that "First Thursday in the Pearl" was an event for local makers to sell their products and had become quite popular. I loaded up the bus with gear, drove down to NW 13th Ave, and asked if I could be a part of the event.

I was greeted by the director, who said, "If you didn't handmake the product, you can't join." Since technically I didn't handmake my gear—it was printed on screen printing machines in North Portland—she politely asked me to leave.

Bummed, I made a U-turn and found a parking spot as close as I could to the entrance, hoping I could catch some of the foot traffic. I looked to my right, saw a bar, and walked in to ask the owner if it'd be all right if I parked there and tried to sell my tees. He looked out the window, saw the bright teal bus, and said, "Sure!"

I began posting on Instagram about First Thursday and encouraged people to come down and experience the city and this unique art event. In the first month, ten people came; in the second month, there were thirty; and by the end of summer, we had lines of people behind the bus, wanting to buy our new product.

The owner of the bar pulled me aside and suggested that the next year we close the block down and throw an outdoor party and festival.

I was in!

Fast-forward and First Thursday in the Pearl became a huge deal and party for our city. Thousands and thousands of people would fill our block drinking, buying gear, and experiencing the city with their friends. Many people have experienced this event now, but not many know it might never have happened if I hadn't made that U-turn.

***

All summer long, Eli and I would load up the bus and hit as many events as we could. If Portlanders were out experiencing Portland, we wanted to be there. We'd roll up with our bus, set out the tables, and stand for hours and hours trying our best to sell the product. As events went on, people started asking about a retail store, and I knew we were ready to think bigger.

LIFE LESSONS LEARNED

- → Put yourself out there and do uncomfortable things.
- → Start small and grow as you go. Celebrate the small wins.
- → Pay attention to your customers and go where they go.
- → Don't be scared to work hard.
- → Make a U-turn. You never know what awaits.

CHAPTER 14

BRICK AND MORTAR

DURING OUR FIRST SUMMER OF POP-UPS, CUSTOMERS repeatedly asked where our retail store was and if they could come by and grab more gear. I'd reply, "You're looking at it! This is our store for now, but do you think we should have a permanent one?"

Every one of them said yes, and the resounding feeling was that there was more demand for gear than what we were currently supplying.

In February of 2015, I called the only person I knew who did real estate, and we began looking at places in order to get a better understanding of cost and whether opening our own spot would even make sense financially. I was experiencing success with the pop-up model, but signing a lease and committing to being open every single day would be a much bigger undertaking.

I had flashbacks to opening my first two offices and how, both times, what started out feeling impossibly expensive ended up working and becoming the step I'd needed to take.

If I was going to take a leap and open a store, I knew it would have to be in a dense and popular part of town that Portlanders frequented. I first looked at NW 23rd, but upon seeing rents north of $10,000 a month, quickly realized that area wouldn't work within my budget. We were offering only a few T-shirt, hat, and sweatshirt options, so I knew we could get by with a small space to start and did not want to bite off more than we could chew.

One option I looked at was next to Providence Park where the Timbers and Thorns played. It was formerly a dry cleaner, and the landlord was offering a really great price to get someone moved in. I knew Portland Gear customers would most likely be Timbers and Thorns fans, and I figured being next to the stadium on busy game days would do well for business.

Upon walking into the space at 627 SW 19th Ave, my first impression wasn't great. In the middle of the space was a big wall that went all the way up to the ceiling, making the 850 square feet feel more like 150. My realtor quickly jumped in and said we could always change the space, knock down walls, paint, and clean, and that we shouldn't worry about or judge it by what it currently looked like.

There was something in the space that caught my eye, though—a dry-cleaner conveyor rack that went all the way up to the ceiling. The rack was empty but already looked awesome. I could envision it full of Portland Gear shirts and drawing people in as an unusual and photo-ready experience.

Scared, but incredibly excited for the future, I signed a five-year lease and decided it was time to take the next big step. I'd bet on myself every time before, and this time felt no different. If it was going to work, it would be because I'd do whatever was needed to see it through. I never once thought about it failing. I just knew in my gut it was going to go well.

Eli and I did most of the build-out ourselves to keep costs down. We bought metal pipes from Home Depot and built racking ourselves, traded @portland Instagram posts for free lighting, and paid a local builder $5,000 to build all the display tables and the checkout station.

As we were getting closer to completion, I needed to think about hours of operation. If I was going to spend all this money and time to open a brick-and-mortar retail experience, I knew it had to be open every day. If someone wanted a Portland Gear shirt at 1 p.m. on a Monday or 5 p.m. on a Sunday, I needed to make sure that could happen.

There was no way I could commit to being open seven days a week and do everything all by myself. I was spending all my time designing clothes; ordering; overseeing photo shoots, pop-ups, and events; handling emails; and growing the business. I needed help. It was time to add my first employee.

Eli had been with me from the beginning and was the logical person to hire. From counting inventory in our apartment to helping at events, he understood my mission for the brand and had been wanting to get more involved. He'd been looking to leave his job, so when I asked, he jumped in. Although I couldn't promise him much money, since I had no clue how much we'd sell, I told him I'd always make sure our rent was taken care of and he'd have a little extra money for beer. He graciously said yes, and it was time to open!

As we were putting the finishing touches on the store, hanging shirts, painting, and planning our opening for the following Saturday, people started to walk in and ask if we were open already. Needing to hustle and start making money, we said yes. Whether we were ready or not, by the end of the first (unplanned) day we were open, we did $5,000 in sales, nearly paying off the entire store's build-out cost.

God was good to me on that day and showed me it was all going to work out. I'd put the time in, slowly growing this audience—from @portland Instagram posts to PDX meetups, the Portland Gear online store, and pop-ups—and I felt the community and I were really ready to make this place a home.

At our opening party, over four hundred people lined up around the building to show their support and purchase gear. We had the most amazing, hectic, and rewarding night in our history and even had a special appearance by my by-then good friend C. J. McCollum of the Blazers.

As I stood outside with the line wrapped around the building behind me, Eli took the photo I'd always dreamed of. A childhood vision had come true.

LIFE LESSONS LEARNED

- → Listen to your customers.
- → You must risk to experience the reward.
- → Don't think about failure. Plan for success.
- → Community is your lifeblood.
- → Dreams do come true.

CHAPTER 15

LIVING THE DREAM

WITHIN WEEKS OF OPENING THE STORE, I REALIZED I NO longer wanted an investor involved.

Although the initial sum of money had helped purchase the first inventory and the bus, I was always afraid to spend my investor's money for fear of losing it. I ran the business very lean and had a good understanding of our inventory needs and margin. It also became quickly apparent that this brand was going to be something I'd want to do for a very long time, and I just didn't have use for all that money right away. I'd be able to grow the business organically by reinvesting the profits.

I realized my investor's 10 percent share of the business could potentially be worth something big, and I didn't feel like he was adding any value to the project. I sent him an email stating that as majority owner of the business, I'd like to buy him out and retain 100 percent of the company. I saw myself one day passing it down to my kids—or being able to grow it in whatever direction I wanted, without always worrying about someone else's best interest. The entire reason I'd started my own business was to carve my own path, and having an investor involved just didn't feel right.

After a few tough phone calls and negotiations, my investor and I agreed on a buyout number, and I purchased the shares back. He made a great return on his short-term investment, and I was able to retain 100 percent of the brand I was working so hard to build.

* * *

Eli and I had been working every day for two straight months and realized it was time to add another employee. One of my high-school friends, Mack, an original Creative 35 member, was about to graduate and move back to PDX and would be looking for work. Like me, he'd done screen printing and graphic design since 2015, and he became a great addition to the team.

From designing graphics to ordering and shipping products, driving the bus to events, working on collaborations, managing photo shoots, events, posts on social media, emails, charitable giving, inventory, and networking, the three of us made it happen. We hustled around the clock and always found a way to have fun while working hard.

Eli and Mack understood the brand, how I wanted to treat people, and what I expected of them as teammates in this growing venture. They began taking a lot of the day-to-day load off of me, which allowed me to focus on growing the business and thinking of creative ways to market it.

LIVING THE DREAM

* * *

In April of 2015, I got a direct message from the @trailblazers official Instagram account: "Our retail department loves the product you guys put out. Interested in selling at the Fan Shop in Moda Center?"

I tried to keep it cool in my response by saying I was open to a meeting and would love to learn more, but inside, young Marcus was giddy.

With a bag of P caps in hand, I walked into the Trail Blazers' front office and was greeted by a gentleman named Kris. They liked what I was doing and wanted to work on an exclusive, small line of products that would be sold as part of their "Locals Corner" inside Moda Center, where the Blazers played.

Yes, you read that right—I had a chance to sell my new brand, Portland Gear, inside Moda Center, where my favorite basketball team played. I left the P caps with everyone in the office as gifts and told them I'd love to be part of their Locals Corner.

A week later, I got a message from Kris saying a few players on the team saw him wearing his hat on the plane and asked how to get one. I gave him half a dozen hats and let him spread them around as he pleased.

The next week on Instagram, I saw one of the Blazers rocking my cap on the plane and sent him a direct message to thank him. To my surprise, he replied and said he'd like to come by the shop sometime and learn more.

At first, I was surprised an NBA player wanted to come to my store, but after having flashbacks to Wesley Matthews visiting, and my days in the Nike Employee Store helping athletes, I knew I had the background and confidence to provide him with a great experience.

I invited him in, and the next day he rolled up. Having an NBA player in my store was a near out-of-body experience. I remember going to games as a kid, hanging over the rail two hours early in hopes of getting an autograph or sweatband, and walking the Nike campus hoping to see someone famous. Now, only ten years later, to have a player in my store, getting to know me as a person, was a highlight of my life.

Since 2015, I've seen Portland Gear on more Trail Blazers, Timbers, Thorns, and other local athletes than I can count. I still feel like a kid every time it happens. Every year, we host an event where I invite players from all the teams into our store for a free autograph session for kids and fans. I view the access and relationships I have to these players as a privilege, and I want to share it with the community. Events like this are something I would have loved to attend as a kid, so now seeing the biggest smiles on the faces of kids in line as they're about to come meet their idols really brings everything full circle for me.

I value my connections, relationships, and reputation more than anything in the world, and having well-known locals and athletes know, wear, and appreciate the brand is humbling. Going from being a local kid loving all these teams to now having personal relationships with the players, coaches, and front offices constantly reminds me that what we're creating has always been and will always be about the people first.

LIFE LESSONS LEARNED

- → Don't be scared to ask for what feels right.
- → Relationships make the world go round.
- → Teamwork makes the dream work.
- → Surround yourself with like-minded people.
- → Uplift those who uplift you.

CHAPTER 16

FAINTING

MY PORTLAND GEAR HIGHS WERE HIGH, BUT THE LOWS were also intense. In 2017, I experienced my first fainting episode, and it couldn't have come at a worse time.

Portland Gear was going great, and I was invited to Japan to take part in a new "Portland pop-up shop experience" that Travel Portland was hosting. I'd never taken a business trip for my company and was thrilled by this opportunity. I was approved to bring one person with me, which meant Eli would be joining, and we'd get to experience this together.

All the products were shipped in advance, tickets and hotels booked, translators ready to pick us up from the airport, and a fun two-week itinerary was in hand.

After checking and double-checking our flights, we arrived at the airport for our Tuesday morning flight at 7 a.m. When I got to the self-help kiosk to begin checking our bags, the machine wouldn't recognize our ticket numbers. Starting to feel nervous, I frantically checked my emails to find my confirmation number.

I got in line to speak with the service representative and, after presenting my number, was informed our flight had departed the previous day.

My heart dropped.

"No, no—I've been checking this flight info every day for weeks," I replied.

"We emailed you three months ago and let you know that due to scheduling conflicts the flight was moved up a day. You should have received an email."

I remembered seeing an email from Delta months earlier, but I hadn't made anything of it; I'd thought it was one of the spam emails I often got. Even though I did receive their email, the flight date did not update in my calendar, which was what I'd been looking at.

As I stood at the counter, the lights started to feel really warm.

I began panicking, knowing a translator was waiting for us in Japan and I had no way of reaching out to warn them we'd be late. The thought of this person waiting in the airport for hours on end made me feel extremely anxious.

I tried calling my rep at Travel Portland, and Eli took off running to find our friend who worked at another airline to try and book a different flight. Delta said we could fly out the

FAINTING

next day, but that didn't solve my problem—there were people expecting us.

My body was getting warmer and warmer, and my vision began to narrow. Suddenly, the glow of the lights was laser-sharp, and the next thing I knew, I came back to consciousness looking up at the ceiling with concerned faces looking down at me.

I had fainted.

The people behind me sat me up on the scale and told me I'd collapsed and hit my head on the counter on the way down.

Eli came running back and was confused to see me down.

I was confused, too.

As I sat there for a few minutes getting my bearings, I quickly remembered that someone would be waiting for us in Japan, and we needed to book a flight to get there as soon as possible. I didn't want to disappoint them.

I figured fainting was from low blood sugar, so I chugged Gatorade, ate sour skittles, and booked a full new flight for $5,000. We would head to Seattle first and then to South Korea and Japan, making the trip eight hours longer.

Eli and I took off sprinting through the airport, sweating profusely and intermittently chugging Gatorade, and we made it to the plane right as the doors were closing.

"What even happened to you?" he said.

"I have no clue, but we'll never forget this." Little did I know this episode would be the start of a struggle with anxiety.

After an incredibly long two days of travel, we finally made it to Japan and could begin our journey. We planned to spend five days in Osaka for the pop-up and the remaining ten days traveling by bullet train to see as much of Japan as we could.

During our time in Osaka, Eli and I would get up early in the morning, walk the city streets, grab a rice breakfast from 7-Eleven, and jump on the train to arrive at our pop-up by opening.

While selling our Portland Gear next to other Portland vendors, we began getting strange looks from some of the Japanese event directors. I noticed the lead who had helped plan the event start pacing back and forth in front of our booth for hours on end. I felt totally uncomfortable and finally asked him what was wrong.

He pulled me aside and asked for a private word. He proceeded to berate me for fifteen minutes in front of customers and other pop-up employees for taking breaks during the day, having our water bottles in the pop-up, and checking our phones to see if there was anything back home we were missing.

"How dare you not know these Japanese customs? You should have done research before you came over here on a work trip. You're just a young business owner, and there's a reason many of you fail in your first few years—you have no clue how to do anything. You may think your business is cool, but in a few years, no one will remember you and your business will be done."

He made sure that I—a young, American business owner with zero international experience—knew all the things we were doing to disrespect the Japanese retail customs.

My frail emotions and I walked into the bathroom, shut the door, and began bawling. I hated the feeling of being in trouble, especially for something I legitimately didn't know I was doing wrong. It would've been different if someone had pulled us aside and told us not to do these things or helped explain why they were considered disrespectful; but when the first clue we were given was a massive list of everything we did wrong and why we were failures, it was hard to hear.

Over the next three days, I found myself in small back rooms with the leaders from the store, having mediations about what happened and how we could be better.

I was humiliated.

As the pop-up was coming to an end, Eli and I still had a few days to explore and experience this beautiful country. I remember zipping past Mt. Fuji on the bullet train, eating fresh sushi in the Tsukiji fish market, feeding deer in Nara, and visiting an Onitsuka Tiger store.

Before starting Nike, Phil Knight had begun by importing Tigers, so seeing those stores made me feel connected to my roots. I remember reading all of Phil's Japan stories in his book *Shoe Dog*, and I felt like I was walking right behind him in his steps.

I bought matching pairs for Noelle and me and headed home.

LIFE LESSONS LEARNED

→ Double-check your flights.
→ Only worry about things you can control.
→ Do your research on international customs.
→ Go see the world.
→ Understand you're always a work in progress.

CHAPTER 17

ANXIETY AND INSECURITIES

WHEN I ARRIVED BACK IN THE STATES, I HAD A ROUTINE doctor appointment, including vaccines. After receiving the first shot, I looked down and was surprised to find a small bubble under my skin.

As my vision began to narrow again, my breathing slowed, and my next memory was waking up with the nurses looking down at me, worried. They said I'd fainted and fallen backward, almost onto the open needles.

This was now the second time in two weeks I had fainted, and I began thinking something must be wrong with me. I asked the nurses why this was happening and what I should do to prevent it. The only advice they gave was to stay hydrated, make sure my blood sugar was never too low, and that if I started feeling like that again, to sit down with my head between my legs and get low to the ground.

As soon as I left, I started feeling anxious about when this was going to happen again and what was causing it—which brings me to the story at the beginning of the book.

A few days after the doctor visit, while presenting to three hundred students at the University of Portland, I had my first full-on panic attack. After faking the leg cramp, running sprints in the park, and crying all night long, I spent the next day looking again for open doctor appointments so I could get myself fixed.

Sitting in a sterile, bright white office at age twenty-five with tears rolling down my face, I told the doctor: "I don't know what's happening to me and why I keep fainting, but I don't like how it makes me feel, and I want it to stop."

He said I was experiencing anxiety and that the "best approach" was to begin taking anti-anxiety medication and to participate in talk therapy. I didn't want to do either, but I also didn't like how I was feeling, so I agreed.

After starting the medication, my body began feeling slow, unadjusted, and plain under the weather. I became moody and irritable and wasn't acting or feeling like myself.

Usually an extremely extroverted person, I now found myself staying in, blinds closed, lights off, and not wanting to talk or deal with anyone. I chose a therapist and began sessions every two weeks but found it hard to truly open up and accomplish anything within the one-hour time frame. I also didn't connect with the therapist well, and the sessions felt very transactional. I was willing to dig in deep, but right when I would get close to uncovering something, our time would be up and it would have to wait.

ANXIETY AND INSECURITIES

* * *

Since fainting for the first time in 2017, I've been on a quest to understand my mind, body, and soul so I can better serve my employees, wife, family, and community.

After six months of feeling poorly on the medication, I weaned myself off. It might have made me feel a little better, but the side effects hadn't been a fair trade. Through lots of hard work in therapy and reading books, I realized these episodes were a way of my body begging me to pay attention because my emotional balance was off.

Earlier that year, Noelle and I had moved into a condo above the Portland Gear store so I could always be working and maximize my time to grow Portland Gear. After a few months of living in our 700-square-foot condo, I began feeling uneasy about never truly being able to "turn off."

Even when I was trying to unplug, I'd have to walk by my office on the way out of the building, which made me feel like I was always going to work. Inevitably, there would be an employee with a question or a visitor I'd want to say hi to, so I'd walk in. Even if it was for only ten seconds to say hi, it felt like I'd crossed the threshold and gone to work, thus negating a true day off and breaking the boundary I was needing. Since 2012, I'd also been on my phone all day and all night building my businesses and social media pages, and I was now feeling the lack of phone-free alone time. Technology has us more connected than ever, and this idea of "always on" was weighing on me. Creating content for social media, posting across every platform multiple times a day, writing captions, replying to all the comments, designing products, emailing, planning future projects, handling finances and leases, and overseeing a growing team all quickly became overwhelming.

Simply put, over the last few years I'd lost all separation between my personal and professional lives, and my body was crying out for help.

What I thought would be a blessing—living close—turned out to be detrimental to my health. This lack of boundary, the sudden growth of Portland Gear, and a wedding on the horizon resulted in my mind and body having a hard time finding peace.

Realizing the condo wasn't serving my mental health, Noelle and I moved out, and I began intentionally creating separation and boundaries. It wasn't easy, but it was necessary.

I read an article by local NBA player Kevin Love that really spoke to me. He shared about his panic attack and how he'd been suffering silently from anxiety for years. Everyone knew Kevin as a basketball player, but after his article came out, they got to know him as a human. Knowing him personally, I sent a message thanking him for his bravery in speaking out. I also decided to write and share something of my own.

I stayed up late one night writing everything I'd been experiencing and put it into a blog on the Portland Gear website. I immediately started receiving emails, texts, and calls from peers and customers who were experiencing something similar. It felt freeing to express what I was going through, and I noticed that the more I shared and talked about it, the more it gave others the confidence to share about themselves. It was like a chain reaction.

ANXIETY AND INSECURITIES

The same curator of TEDxPortland, David Rae, was helping the University of Oregon host a Presidential Speaker series called "Wings" in Portland. After reading my letter, he thought it would be good to share my story to his audience of two hundred Portlanders.

Still worried about speaking in public due to my fear of fainting, I told him I would do it, but under one condition: that I could sit in a chair onstage.

With a packed house in the auditorium and my parents in the fifth row, I anxiously paced in the hallway until it was my time to share. Before writing my blog, besides Noelle and a few close employees, I'd never opened up to anyone about what I was going through. My parents and peers would hear all of this for the first time, and while I was scared to be vulnerable and disappoint them, I knew it was something I needed to do for myself.

Sitting in the chair onstage that night, I held nothing back. I shared my truths and that there was more to me than what people may see on social media or hear about around town. I, too, was a human who experienced very normal and human things. I received so much positivity and love after I got off stage that it felt like I'd just discovered a new gift—to share with others more than just the cool Portland Gear things they see, but also the vulnerable and raw emotions that I and other business owners experience.

After all those events, I decided to really invest more in my body and a better understanding of the things that had been making me unravel. I realized pretty quickly that some of the insecurities

I'd been carrying around since my teen years were still weighing on my subconscious.

Growing up, I was always one of the shortest kids in school and would often get teased. As a freshman in high school, I was five-foot-three and wouldn't get my braces off until I was done with my junior year. Wanting to play basketball and be competitive like my friends, I tried out and made JV Two, the lowest level. Our squad consisted of freshmen, sophomores, and juniors—every one of them taller and more developed than me.

I legitimately looked like the team ball boy in our photo.

Although I tried my hardest not to care, I became increasingly insecure about my height. All I wanted was to be the same size as all my friends and be able to play competitively at their level, but I had not hit a decent growth spurt yet.

My parents took me to a specialist at OHSU, where I had blood work and x-rays done to test my growth plates. The doctor said everything was fine and normal, but that I'd be a late bloomer and might not grow for a few more years. He said I'd always look about three years younger than I was and that I could take weekly growth hormone shots if I wanted to speed up the process.

Although in high school I had more friends than I could count, and was always on the Homecoming court, deep down all I wanted to do was be able to bench-press a forty-five-pound plate on each side and be the same shape and size as all my friends. Sounds silly, I know, but that was really important to me at the time.

Thankfully, after a family discussion, we elected not to do the shots; but my parents were willing to explore it more if it was something that I really felt I needed to try. The next year, I did end up hitting that growth spurt, but it was too late to ever get to play the sports I'd wanted to like my peers or look my age in high school or college.

One thing that didn't have a hard time growing was my nose. Although it's a Harvey family trait, I started feeling increasingly insecure about it in my later years of high school and into college. With the support of my wife, I made a personal decision in 2021 to have a nose job and change my appearance. Even though I was happily married with a spouse who loved me exactly as I was, and I felt confident in the person I was, I'd look in the mirror and wonder what it'd feel like to have a regular-shaped nose.

Being a person of faith, I wrestled with the idea that God made me this way for a reason and that I shouldn't be wanting to change who I was born to be. After a conversation with my parents and Noelle, who all said go for it, I booked the surgery. I'm happy with the results.

It's interesting to look at yourself in the mirror for the first time and see someone new staring back. Although it did change a bit of my self-talk, at my core I realized I'm the exact same person and that physical appearance doesn't change what really matters in life, like how I treat people, what I do for others, and how I love myself.

The self-work I've done over the past few years has been hard but also incredibly freeing. I started working out again, reading books, visiting a chiropractor and a therapist, drinking more water; and I even got a puppy, which has helped make me a more present and in-the-moment person.

I've learned that everyone is going through something and that our past really does affect our present and future. It gets messy and uncomfortable to go backward and face things you've been running from, but it's how I believe confidence and peace are found.

Start now. Invest in your body, seek balance, and give yourself the opportunity to chase your passions and desires without any restraints. Life is short—love what you do, surround yourself with great people, challenge yourself to get better at things you enjoy, and be sure to leave an impact on others that can make their lives easier.

CHAPTER 18

WHERE WE ARE

THE THING I'M MOST PROUD OF SINCE STARTING PORT-land Gear in 2014 is our team and the reputation we have within the city. The people behind Portland Gear are the heartbeat of the brand, and it's my joy to evolve with them all as we continue to expand. Portland Gear quickly became bigger than me, and if it wasn't for the hard work and commitment of my employees, it wouldn't have been able to grow as it has. Within the first year, we shipped an order to every state and nearly sixty-five countries around the world, with notable collaborations and partnerships within the city itself.

After a few years of working on our individual projects and going our own ways, Wookie and I reconnected in 2019 and expressed our desires to work together again. We always enjoyed being around each other, and when the opportunity came for me to bring him onto the Portland Gear team to lead our product and apparel design, it was a no-brainer. I'm incredibly thankful to have him as a part of our team, not only mentoring our younger staff but also elevating our brand and product to a level I never thought we'd make it to. It's great having a loyal partner like him back in my corner.

Zack Dean is another standout at Portland Gear that the brand is lucky to have. I first met Zack at Saturday Market where he was selling his own shirts in 2015. He was a current student at Tigard High School and invited me to come into his class to speak a few times. Zack was also the student leader when I had my panic attack at the University of Portland. On Black Friday 2016, he came early to our retail store and offered to help. The line of people was much longer than anticipated and we needed extra hands, so I let him jump in. I put him to work with zero training, and he was a natural.

By the end of the day, a handful of customers had come up and said, "That Zack employee of yours was so kind. That was the best customer service I've ever received! How long has he worked for you?"

"He just showed up this morning and technically doesn't even work here, but thanks!" I replied, laughing.

After the madness died down that night, I asked Zack if he'd want to come and help run the retail store. He said yes and has been working, grinding, and growing with us ever since.

Sean is another awesome human who's been in our orbit since the original PDX MEET days, where I'd have him do cardistry for people as entertainment. Just a kid, Sean was incredible behind the camera and produced content that was distinctive and thoughtful. The day he graduated from Portland State, I called and asked Sean if he'd like to join the team, and he couldn't have said yes faster. Starting in the store like everyone does, Sean has grown immensely over the years and is a big reason our social pages and video content look as engaging and professional as they do. His eye for photo and video, and his wit, make our brand feel approachable and relatable to Portlanders of all ages. There's no limit to what Sean will continue to do for Portland Gear over the years, and I'm excited to see it unfold.

I want to employ people at Portland Gear who think differently and aren't scared to put in the work. I want an environment where everyone feels empowered, valued, and part of our growing community and knows that their ideas matter. We've been able to deepen our roots in the community and make a name for ourselves by treating people right; servicing the people of Portland through events, collaborations, and nonprofit support; and making cool and inclusive products that people are proud to wear.

The cornerstone event I'm most proud of creating is our summer internship program called "Brand Camp." I saw a need for real-world learning experiences for students aged sixteen through twenty-two and designed an engaging and fun program for them to experience.

Every summer, we host high school- and college-aged students in our downtown office for a week of team building, learning, working on client projects, games, and fun. The camp is divided into groups, where they're pressed to work on real-world projects for local businesses and present their solutions at the end of the week. We also take a field trip around town to show how clothes are made, meet with up-and-coming companies, and provide moments where these students can gain clarity regarding their goals and what they want to do with their young lives. It's my goal to push them outside of their comfort zone and find something interesting they never knew existed—something that might spark joy.

We've reached hundreds of kids through our program, and we hire a majority of our retail staff from this pool of students. The camp is just one of the ways we stay invested in our community and help inspire the next wave of young entrepreneurial-thinking Portlanders who will shape the city into the future.

* * *

One of my pinch-me moments happened on a random Thursday in the spring of 2018. I was working from a coffee shop a mile away on my off day when I received a text from Mack. He told me that Tinker Hatfield, the greatest footwear designer of all time—creator of a number of Air Jordan shoes and even the Oregon O—was currently standing in my store.

Mack had seen him walking by outside but wasn't sure it was actually him, so he ran out and yelled "Tinker!" hoping he'd turn around. His hunch was right, and Tinker turned around and walked into the store.

Mack texted "Tinker," and I knew what it meant. I threw my computer in my bag and took off running as fast as I could, pretending I was sprinting the backstretch at Hayward Field. Things were flying out of my bag, but I didn't have time to slow down or grab them because I wanted to meet one of my lifelong idols. Mack stalled him for nine minutes until I flew into the shop, out of breath, and introduced myself.

We all had a good laugh.

Besides Phil Knight, Tinker Hatfield was one of the most important and inspiring people in my life. What he created and designed at Nike were things that shaped my childhood. I began telling him our story, selling him on the idea of Portland Gear, and showing him our office and space around the corner. I shared how inspiring I thought he was, and that it was a true honor to have him in my place of business.

Standing in our messy office full of boxes, I could tell he felt comfortable and almost nostalgic about his days at Nike. I wondered if even, somehow, he saw a bit of his younger self in me.

As our thirty-minute conversation drew to a close, I asked if I could send him home with gear as a thank you. He replied, "You've got a fan in me now; this is a cool logo!"

Validation again.

Now, years later, I still see photos of Tinker wearing P caps, and I've had the honor and pleasure of staying in contact with him and being able to call him a mentor.

* * *

From becoming personal friends with countless Trail Blazers, Timbers, Thorns, and Winterhawks players who rock our gear to collaborating with Widmer Brothers, TEDxPortland, Breakside Brewing, OHSU, Water Ave Coffee, Stoller Family Estate, University of Oregon, Good Coffee, Draplin Design Co., and local high schools, serving on nonprofit boards, and more, we've made a commitment to our community and wake up every day with a mindset of service.

Portland Gear is a brand made for people to wear and share their pride, and we're honored to get to do that every day. Our yearly anniversary sale sees as many as three thousand people lined up around the building in support, and we've created events for the city that people participate in and enjoy feeling like a part of the fabric of where they live.

From Eli to Zack, Wookie, Sean, and Wanda to the list of amazing retail employees and staff who've come and gone, a sincere thank you for constantly putting your best foot forward and allowing me to live out a childhood dream. There's nothing like growing something from the ground up with great people and feeling like the work we do truly matters. I'm fortunate to feel this way every day.

Our goal is to bring this city together and have people believe in it and love it as much as we do. I'm constantly excited about the future that awaits us. I hope Portland Gear is just as relevant, if not more, in a hundred years as it is today. It really feels like sometimes we're still just getting started.

There are thousands of stories from these years that will come out in time, but creating this book now and documenting my journey so far is something I'll cherish for the rest of my life. I do believe this is just the start of our story and hope and pray that Portland Gear becomes a generational brand. I want my daughter to work here one day and continue a legacy born out of a simple desire to wear Portland and harness the pride of Rose City.

For my mother's belief, my sister's support, my dad's first order, Noelle's love, employees who believed, and the thousands of customers that rep our gear all over the world, thank you for believing in small business, and thank you for wearing this brand for our city.

I am a product of all of you.

www.ingramcontent.com/pod-product-compliance
Lightning Source LLC
Chambersburg PA
CBHW030526080526
44586CB00011B/335